PROFILES IN FAITH

Discovering Baptist Beginnings

Bruce Reed Pullen

A Travel Journal

Copyright © 2006 by Bruce Reed Pullen

ISBN 0-7414-3438-5

Published by:

PUBLISHING.COM

1094 New DeHaven Street, Suite 100
West Conshohocken, PA 19428-2713
Info@buybooksontheweb.com
www.buybooksontheweb.com
Toll-free (877) BUY BOOK
Local Phone (610) 941-9999
Fax (610) 941-9959

Printed in the United States of America

Printed on Recycled Paper

Published August 2006

DEDICATION

This book is dedicated to my family

my wife

JUDITH

my daughters

BONNIE AND BETH

Bonnie's husband

MICHAEL

and our grandchildren

BRITTANY AND SETH

and my spiritual family

the people who call themselves

BAPTISTS

Contents

Profiles in Faith

Discovering Baptist Beginnings

PART THREE – EPILOGUE

PREFACE

The abbey at Iona in Scotland

Within one hundred years after Jesus' began his ministry the Christian faith had reached Britain. With the invasion of the Roman army came the wives and traders, educators and evangelists, who brought this new belief to Britain. When the army began leaving three hundred years later to defend Rome, the native Celts nurtured the faith in a form influenced by their culture. They formed a way of witnessing to their faith which today we call Celtic Christianity. In *Discovering Celtic Christianity* I wrote about the Celtic saints and their sites, their roots, relationships, and relevance. That book discusses pilgrimage and then combines stories of these saints and of visits to their sites such as Iona.

On a later trip to Britain, we visited sites associated with the start of the Separatist movement. Discontent over the long control of worship by the state churches, first Roman and then

Anglican, initiated the movement. In the American colonies Separatists evolved as Congregational, Baptist, Presbyterian, and Methodist churches, so my wife and I also visited sites associated with early Baptists in America.

Profiles in Faith - Discovering Baptist Beginnings is about Baptist saints and their sites, their roots and their people. The Prologue highlights the history of the creative Celtic period that very much laid the foundation for the Separatist movement. The Profiles focus on a few of the personalities who led a revival of the faith and planted new congregations. The Epilogue concludes with some reflections on the continuing revival these persons started.

The faith of such famous personalities as Roger Williams and Charles Spurgeon is profiled along with those who are less known such as John Myles and John Clarke. The issues with which they wrestled, such as passing on their faith to those who had no faith in Jesus and gaining and maintaining religious liberty, are issues that still confront us today. The tensions between conformists and nonconformists are still with us. People desire religious liberty, yet others seek to limit that liberty. People desire separation of church and state and yet others seek to use civil government to promote faith issues. It is my hope that this book will help keep alive our collective memory as Baptists.

Each chapter closes with reflections that may be used for a meditative moment. A discussion guide is found in the appendix. All photos included are mine.

Special thanks to my wife, Judith Gunnemann Pullen, for her encouragement and company on my travels in Britain. I am especially grateful for the editorial skills of Diane J. Shearer who both contributed to and edited my first book and who in editing this book has significantly sharpened the focus and form of *Profiles in Faith - Discovering Baptist Beginnings*.

Dr. Bruce Reed Pullen
12 College Park Lane
Westfield, MA 01085

Cover: The American Baptist Center
in Valley Forge, Pennsylvania

INTRODUCTION

John Hart memorial.
The First Baptist Church, Hopewell, New Jersey

WELCOME HOME

I was born in Princeton, New Jersey, half-way between Hightstown, where I grew up, and Hopewell, where my grandparents lived. We traveled there frequently for family gatherings. Years later, after graduating from seminary, I was called to be pastor of Calvary Baptist Church in Hopewell. I was home. My family could trace their roots back to the founding family, the Stouts.

I was also at home in the little Baptist church for my spiritual roots lay in the Baptist family. Just down the street was one of the oldest Baptist churches in the country and in its cemetery was a monument to John Hart, the only Baptist to sign the Declaration of Independence.

Home is that special place in our mind and heart, a particular place furnished in a specific way and inhabited by specific people. It's a place where we belong. Where do you belong? What are your roots? Who are the people you admire? How have they influenced your life? If you are a Christian, you are part of God's family and your spiritual roots may be traced back through your church to the first disciples. You may have considered visiting those places where Jesus walked with his disciples. Often we find these are "thin places" where the wall between us and God is "thinner"[1] and the visit becomes life transforming. Pilgrimage, travel that transforms our lives, occurs when, as we explore our spiritual roots, we link saints and their sites.

FAMILY OF GOD

The Bible comes alive for us when we put ourselves into its stories. We are there with Mary and Joseph as they return to the family home in Bethlehem where they created a place in the manger for baby Jesus because the house where they were staying was so crowded.

Jesus came to invite us to be part of an extended family, the family of God. You have a place in the family of God, a place where you belong. When our spiritual family gathers, when we worship God together, when we share the bread and the cup and sing our favorite hymns, we reaffirm our roots, the legacy left by the pioneers of our particular branch of God's family tree.

A BRANCH OF MY FAMILY TREE

On a warm August day in 1971 the Stout family gathered for a reunion in the village of Hopewell, New Jersey. The Stout family traces its roots back to Jonathan Stout and his family who moved to Hopewell in 1706 and further back to Richard and Penelope (Vanprincis) Stout.[2]

As the new pastor I was invited to attend the reunion. The long genealogy charts were carefully laid out on several tables for all to see. Bill Stout, the convener of the clan, jokingly suggested that there were so many names listed that mine might be among them. Much to our surprise, it was. The Reed family can be traced back on my mother's side to William Reed (1689-1762) who settled in the area early in 1700. Reeds have lived in the area ever since, and somewhere along the line a Reed married a Stout.

Around 1620 eighteen-year-old Penelope Vanprincis and her husband sailed from Holland for New Amsterdam (New

York). When their ship foundered on Sandy Hook, the crew and passengers started walking to their destination. Her husband, hurt in the wreck, was unable to keep up with the others. Resting in the woods, they were attacked by natives who killed her husband and left her to die. Penelope awoke with a fractured skull, a left shoulder hacked so that she never regained full use, and a cut across her abdomen. After seven days of living off the land, two natives discovered her. The older one carried her to his home and treated her wounds. After she recovered, he took her to New Amsterdam and there Penelope met and married Richard Stout, an Englishman. They had seven sons and three daughters. Penelope lived to be 110.

In 1686 The Lenni-Lenape tribe invited Jonathan, her third son, to visit them in the area that is now called Hopewell, New Jersey. Twenty years later, he relocated there with his family. By 1715 Jonathan Stout gathered a group and formed the First Baptist Church in his home. By 1747 a Baptist meeting house was built in the valley on land donated by John Hart, a signer of the Declaration of Independence. Under the leadership of Isaac Eaton (1748-72), the church became one of the foremost Baptist churches in the colonies. Although the congregation has dissolved, the meeting house is still there surrounded by a graveyard which includes a monument to John Hart.

Calvary Baptist Church is just down the street from the old meeting house. Many years have passed since that day in August when I discovered my family roots could be traced back to Penelope Stout and to the old Baptist meeting house in Hopewell.

GENEALOGY

Tracing family roots is detective work. You will discover conflicting information from various sources. Often this comes from differing dates or spellings of names. You will interview many sources. Your notebook will become filled with names, places, and dates of births, marriages and deaths. Most of all there will be the family stories. Eventually you will want to visit some of the places where past generations lived, experience the moment, and then capture the impressions with a camera and in a notebook.

This book is about the people who were part of my faith family tree. I learned their stories and visited the places where they were educated or where they ministered.

SOAKING UP IMPRESSIONS

David McCullough, a 1993 Pulitzer Prize winner for his biography of Harry S. Truman, recently wrote a biography of John Adams. In order to understand Adams, McCullough spent hours in the Adams home in Quincy, Massachusetts, soaking up impressions. He also visited the places Adams lived in Europe, immersing himself in Adams's favorite authors, handling Adams's actual letters and diaries as much as he could, and dining in Colonial Williamsburg just as Jefferson and Adams might have done. "It may seem peripheral and amateurish," McCullough say, "but I gotta go smell the place and see how the light comes into a room. . . . It's what I have to do to get myself into their lives and their time."[3]

I saw the places where these early Baptists lived and studied, worshiped where they worshiped, and read from books they wrote. *Profiles in Faith - Discovering Baptist Beginnings*, is the result. I invite you to join me on this pilgrimage as together we discover Baptist beginnings in Britain and America. Let's go exploring!

Dr. Bruce Reed Pullen
brpabc@aol.com

Window in the Chapel at Little Gidding, England

PART ONE

PROLOGUE

"What is past is prologue"

William Shakespeare

"I believe the people of God in history
live in a tension between an ideal
- the universal communion of saints -
and the specific
- the particular people in a definite time and place.
The church's mission in time calls for institutions:
special rules, special leaders, special places.
But when institutions themselves obstruct
the spread of the gospel rather than advancing it,
then movements of renewal arise
to return to the church's basic mission
in the world."[1]

Bruce L. Shelley, Church Historian

TIME LINE

The Romans (42-410)

42-3   Roman army invades Celtic Britain.

100-200   Christian house churches form in Britain

410   Legions withdraw from Britain.
                Christianity spreads to Ireland (Patrick, 432);
                    Iona, Scotland (Columba, 563); and Lindisfarne
                    in northern England (Aidan, 635).

The Saxons and Danes (410-1066)

597   Augustine starts a Roman Catholic mission in
                    southern England at Canterbury.

664   The Synod convenes at Whitby. Celtic and Roman
                    ways clash; Rome consolidates its power.

731   Bede writes *The Ecclesiastical History of the
                    English People.*

871-99   Alfred the Great, Winchester, unifies the English
                    against Vikings in the north.

The Normans (1066-1154)

1066   William and his army defeat the descendants of the
                    Celts, Romans, and Saxons.

The Plantagenet Kings (1154-1485)

1154-89   Henry II restores order in a ravaged country.

1167   Oxford University founded;
                    Cambridge follows in 1209.

1170   Archbishop Thomas Becket murdered in
                    Canterbury Cathedral.

1215	King John (1199-1216) signs the Magna Carta paving the way for Parliament.
1380	John Wyclif (1310-84) translates portions of the Bible into English.
1477	William Caxton prints first book in England making the Bible more available.

The Tudor Kings (1485-1603)

1536-40	Henry VIII (1509-47) takes control of the churches, dissolves monasteries, divorces Catherine and marries Anne Boleyn who gives birth to Elizabeth.
1526	William Tyndale translates New Testament which is banned in Britain.
1549	Edward VI (1547-53). First Book of Common Prayer issued.
1553-8	Mary I tries to restore Catholicism. Anglican bishops burned at the stake.
1558-1603	Elizabeth I restores Anglicanism. Calvinism takes root in Scotland.

The Stuart Kings and the Commonwealth (1603-1714)

1611	James I (1603-25) authorizes new Bible translation
1612	**Thomas Helwys** (1570-1615) organizes the first Baptist church in Britain. James jails him.
1620	The Pilgrims sail from Plymouth on the *Mayflower* and settle in New England.
	Hanserd Knollys (1598-1691) serves churches in New Hampshire and London.
	Roger Williams (1608-83) gathers a Baptist Church in Providence, Rhode Island.
	John Clarke (1609-96) gathers a Baptist Church in Newport, Rhode Island.

1642-49	Civil War. Charles I (1625-49) attempts to rule without Parliament.
	Henry Dunster (1612-58) becomes first President of Harvard.
1649-60	Cromwell establishes Commonwealth in which free churches flourish.
	John Myles (1621-83) forms the first Baptist churches in Wales and then Massachusetts.
	John Bunyan (1628-88), writes *Pilgrim's Progress.*
	Charles II (1660-85) restores Anglican churches, curbs free churches.
	Benjamin Keach (1640-1704) introduces hymn singing to congregations.
	James II (1685-88) creates pro-Catholic policies that sink the ship of state.
1689-1702	Protestants William III and Mary accept the throne.
1792	**Andrew Fuller** (1754-1815) begins Baptist Missionary Society.
	Charles Haddon Spurgeon (1834-92). The "Prince of Preachers."

John Bunyan's Tomb at Bunhill Fields, London

Celtic Roots

Christianity Comes to Britain

The earliest image of Jesus in Britain, British Museum

THE CHRISTIAN FAITH COMES TO BRITAIN

The Christian faith made its way to Britain with the Roman army which invaded in 43 AD and conquered the Celts who lived there. With the army came families and friends, adventuresome traders, and enthusiastic evangelists. As the faith spread, native Celts converted, and pockets of Christian presence were created. They first met in homes where the above mosaic portrait of Jesus was found. It is now on display at the British Museum.

The early churches were Roman at first but were soon influenced by Celtic customs. "Two major figures in the early history of Christianity, a likeable heretic, Pelagius, and a proselytizing saint, Patrick, were born in Britain."[1]

In 313 Constantine, first a general in York and then emperor of the Roman empire, issued an edict that granted to all Christians equal liberty with the older religions. In 314 three British bishops (York, London, and Lincoln) took part in a council at Arles, France.

By 410 the Roman army was leaving, recalled to Rome. As they left, the pagan Angles, Jutes, and Saxons invaded Britain driving the Celts into Cornwall, Wales, Scotland, and Ireland where they kept the faith alive. David in Wales, Patrick in Ireland, Columba in Scotland, and Aidan in Northern England planted Christianity so deeply it would never be uprooted again.

A DIFFERENT ROMAN INVASION

Two hundred years later Bertha, a Parisian princess and a Roman Catholic, came to Canterbury in Kent to marry its pagan king, Ethelbert. Ethelbert soon hosted a mission of 20-30 monks from Rome led by Augustine, a high level administrator and friend of Pope Gregory. Ethelbert invited them to stay, and by June 597 he had become a baptized Christian. By November ten thousand followed the lead of their king and were baptized, some in the River Stour. A thankful pope designated Augustine the Archbishop of the English. St. Martin's church was their temporary headquarters until the abbey, named after Peter and Paul, and later renamed after Augustine, was built. Canterbury Cathedral stands nearby on the site of Christ's Church.

As archbishop, Augustine wrote Gregory asking for counsel on his mission. Gregory advised him that if he found things pleasing to God in the local ritual practices, he should adopt whatever would work to further the gospel. This wise advice was ignored causing a collision with the Celtic Christians whose customs differed from those advocated by Rome. To the Celts the stern and haughty Augustine was just another foreign prelate trying to dictate how they should worship God.

Augustine planted the Roman Catholic way. It eventually clashed with the Celtic Christians in the north. Rome had begun insisting on absolute authority and conformity, a demand the Celtic communities resisted. Finally in 664 Oswy, King of Northumbria, called a council in what is now Whitby to resolve the differences. Oswy, married to a Roman Catholic and keen to introduce some harmony into his personal life and his kingdom, ruled in favor of the Roman Catholics. The churches officially accepted the king's decree although Celtic practices continued to be observed in some areas. Local customs were respected and compromises were allowed under a new archbishop, Theodore of Tarsus, as Gregory had once advised.

Although the Celtic way became "the way not taken," the influence of the Celtic Christians is still with us. The Celts recognized the leadership of women. Each religious community had its own order around which it was organized. The abbots associated with each other, exchanging information and giving support. The members participated in a cycle of worship, work, study, and witness. Although the Celtic influence was submerged, it surfaced once again a thousand years later in the form of the free church movement.

TRAVEL NOTES: BRITISH MUSEUM, LONDON.

My wife, Judy, and I flew from New to Old England to begin exploring Baptist beginnings in Britain, beginnings that are rooted in the Roman invasion and the Celtic expansion of Christianity. After arriving at Heathrow from Boston, we drove to the Bonnington, a hotel near the British Museum. From there we walked to the British Museum, London's imposing gray landmark at Great Russell Street with its magnificent Great Court covered with three thousand panes of glass. There we visited the display on "Christianity in Roman Britain."

The display gives evidence of an early Christian presence in Britain. The commonest symbol is the Chi-rho monogram, formed from the two Greek letters "chi and rho" (X and P), the beginning letters in the name of Christ. In time this became the monogram cross. Another sure indication of a Christian presence is the Greek letters "alpha and omega," beginning and end, often found on either side of the monogram. The image of a fish is another Christian symbol often found on jewelry. The Greek word for fish is "ichthus," which contains the first letters of the Greek words meaning, Jesus Christ, Son of God, Savior.

The exhibit includes a large, circular lead tank with the Chi-rho and alpha-omega symbols on it indicating it may have been used as a baptismal font. Wall paintings show figures in prayer that indicate a worship center; and there are silver pieces, some found as recently as 1975, on which the Chi-rho symbol is prominently displayed. Included also is the central roundel (353-5) from a large floor mosaic found in a villa in Dorset in 1964. Behind the head of the central figure is the Chi-Rho monogram clearly indicating it is meant to be a portrait of Jesus. It is said to be the oldest known representation of Christ in existence anywhere.

TRAVEL NOTES: IONA

Patrick successfully led a mission from Britain to Ireland. Later, Columba and several Irish monks sailed from Ireland to Scotland, establishing a beachhead on the tiny Isle of Iona. The Vikings destroyed the mission but the Benedictines eventually established a center there. The abbey and its ruins are moving reminders of these original missions. In the 1930's a movement to restore Iona began which continues today. Although maintenance of the buildings is now under the administration of a trust, worship services continue in the restored abbey.

Judy and I recently visited Iona for several days, staying at Dun Craig, an independent retreat center managed by Jenny McClellan. We enjoyed the cool summer breezes as we walked the many paths and sailed the waters around the isle. We joined in the worship in the abbey and marveled at the varied Celtic crosses on display. Thousands visit the isle every year. If you go, plan to stay over at least one night.

TRAVEL NOTES: WALES

In Wales just outside Cardiff, a land of dramatic beauty and ancient legend, we leisurely visited the Museum of Welsh Life, an outdoor display of early Welsh homes that includes the recreation of a Celtic village. A palisade and ditch encircle the compound where three thatched roofed, stonewalled, circular homes stand. Inside the houses are weaving looms and other everyday utensils of the Celts. In Cardiff we thrilled to the music of Cambrensis, a choral group based in Cardiff, at their annual May concert. This Christian chorus joined with a symphony orchestra and two hundred plus choir members from local churches to perform a variety of Christian music.

David, the patron saint of Wales, lived and taught in the area now known as St. Davids. We have been to this rugged area of Wales several times to visit sites associated with David in the city of St. Davids and with Illtud in Llantwit Major. The cathedral in this small city is one of the finest in Britain, well worth a visit. During the last week of May we attended its annual Music Festival in the cathedral.

REFLECTIONS: SHARING OUR FAITH - Luke 10:1-8

Billy Graham, when asked by a reporter why God had chosen him to preach the peace of God, replied, "When I get to heaven, that's the first question I'm going to ask him." We may wonder why God chose us, but we know that with the peace comes both the joy and the responsibility of telling others how they may also experience the peace of God.

Besides the twelve, Jesus had many other disciples, lay people who followed him. He sent them out in teams to tell others what he had taught them. These witnesses were to travel light and move quickly to their destinations. They were to stay in one home, not moving around, while they ministered in the village, blessing and healing the people. Then they were to engage the people in conversation about the coming Kingdom. Jesus warned these disciples not to be surprised if not everyone welcomed their message.

There is a certain realism in Jesus' instructions. Our witness, if gentle and caring, will usually be welcome, but a few will reject it and we should not be surprised. When we meet resistance, we are to move on to another effort and not indulge in prolonged regrets. Jesus also advises us to not be surprised when people accept the gift we share. We are assured that whatever the results are to our witnessing, we can rejoice that our names are recorded in the book of life.

The early church gradually grew by sending teams of two or more to an area to live with the people, to explain what it means to be a disciple, to create a church in the community in which people could worship and study, and then to send a team out to begin the cycle all over again.

Celtic Christianity has its roots in this model. The Celtic monks, often with the permission or invitation of a king, established mission centers in which they cared for the disadvantaged, provided shelter for the traveler, trained minds through ancient manuscripts, worked the land, and provided faithful witness in pagan areas. These mission centers are models for today's congregations seeking to minister to an unchurched world.

9

They were ministering to pagans, non-believers, who had no idea what it meant to belong to a Christian community and to believe in Jesus as Lord and Savior, and so are we. They found the key to sharing our faith is first developing a dialogue within a welcoming environment. Only then may we share in words, easily understood, how faith in Jesus impacts our lives. Renewed life for ourselves and our churches depends on enabling people to become disciples, those who belong and believe, so they may in turn witness to the faith they hold.

CLOSING

A Prayer in the Celtic Trinitarian tradition

God, guide me on the way;
Jesus, give me life forever with you;
Holy Spirit, fill me with joy.
Open my eyes to your coming; my ears to your calling;
and my hands to your caring.
In the name of the God who comes to us in three persons,
blessed Trinity. Amen

THE CROSS AND THE CROWN

The site where Thomas Beckett was martyred

CHURCH AND STATE

Baptists have been noted for their life-long struggle for the
separation of church and state and for the freedom of the individual
to choose a way to worship. In contrast, the church in Rome sought
to standardize and then control the way the faith was practiced. The
sacraments touch everyone from birth to death so that the threat of
being barred from them (excommunication) was a powerful force in
making Christians conform. As the power of the church grew, the
secular authorities, the kings, clashed with it.

Henry II, in an attempt to extend his power over British churches, had his friend Thomas Beckett, then Chancellor of England, elected Archbishop of Canterbury in 1162. Beckett surprisingly affirmed the position of the church and was brutally murdered in Canterbury Cathedral on December 29, 1170, by four of Henry's knights. One tradition claims that Henry II, after hearing the news in Normandy, returned to the capital city of Winchester and then traveled to Canterbury. The 120- mile route he may have taken from Winchester to Canterbury has come to be called The Pilgrims' Way. Another pilgrimage route from London to Canterbury was made famous in Chaucer's *Canterbury Tales*.

On June 12, 1215, one of the more dramatic moments in English history occurred at Runnymede. King John and the barons agreed on a Magna Carta (Great Charter) or contract covering how they were to be governed. Two principles were established: certain laws would have greater authority than the king; and, if he did not observe them, the people reserved the right to force him to do so. The foundations for Parliament were thus laid.

By the end of the thirteenth century the churches and monasteries were at the height of their power. Over 600 monasteries existed, creating a wealthy, holy elite living in isolated communal life. Headed by politically appointed bishops who amassed great wealth, the churches gradually divorced themselves from the people. Into the vacuum stepped the "jolly" friars, the Franciscans, who kept in close contact with the people, preaching and leading worship, not in Latin, but in English, French or Italian. A back-to-the-people movement was forming.

In the next century a movement surfaced led by John Wyclif, a professor at Oxford. His teachings, that the supreme test of authority lay not in the churches but in the Bible, "a charter written by God," inspired a religious revival that challenged the authority of the churches. Wyclif translated the Bible into English so people could read it, hear it, and understand it. Because people could now discover a personal relationship with God, excommunication no longer had as powerful a hold over them. But by 1382 the authorities had effectively silenced Wyclif at Oxford so he began sending "poor priests" with a few pages of his English Bible throughout the countryside preaching the Word of God. This revival paved the way for the religious freedom that was soon to surface. Unlike some reformers, he died peacefully at his parish in Lutterworth.

When Henry VIII (1509-1547) came to the throne, new answers were being given to old religious questions: "How are we saved? Where does religious authority lie? What is the church? What is the essence of Christian living?"[1]

Martin Luther in Germany advocated a return to a time when the clergy were guides, pointing out the way to God. Their ministry was to encourage people to study the scriptures and make a personal decision to follow Jesus.

In Zurich (1525) Conrad Grebel baptized George Blaurock, a former priest, upon confession of personal faith in Jesus. Critics called them re-baptizers or Anabaptists. "They (the Anabaptists) were the first Christians in modern times to preach the right to join in worship with others of like faith without state support and without state persecution."[2]

In England Henry VIII, taking a middle-of-the-road approach, had Parliament pass the Act of Supremacy (1534) making the king, not the pope, the head of the Anglican (English) churches. Changes were introduced in worship. English was used, not Latin. An English Bible was adopted. Canon law was overhauled. Relics and images were destroyed. Henry remained Catholic in most of his beliefs, so changes in dogma were only slight; however, the payments to the pope were diverted into the king's coffers. The monasteries, which owned about a sixth of the land in England, were dissolved and their wealth transferred to the crown.

Reform of the churches continued. In 1549 the Book of Common Prayer using English was adopted. Cranmer's writings and Latimer's preaching moved England further from Catholic influence. Queen Mary (1553-8), forced by King Henry, her father, to deny her Catholic faith, sought to return the country to the control of the Catholic tradition.

Persecution was rampant. It was to give her the name, "Bloody Mary." Three hundred men and women, including bishops Cranmer, Latimer, and Ridley, died in the flames of the fires of Smithfield because of their faith. Latimer encouraged Ridley with the now famous words, "Be of good comfort, Master Ridley, and play the man; we shall this day light such a candle by God's grace in England as, I trust, shall never be put out."

Elizabeth soon succeeded to the throne. Under her leadership the Anglican churches adopted a "Middle Way," neither Roman nor radically Protestant. The Act of Uniformity required all Englishmen to conform to the Church of England, which, as an established state church, was just another branch of the government with bishops and policies determined by political authorities. It was during this period that those who wished to further purify the churches, the Puritans, surfaced.

When James was called from Presbyterian Scotland to become king of England, the Puritan movement, demanding simpler church rites and a more Calvinistic theology, saw a ray of hope. In response to their petition, James invited them to a conference at Hampton Court (1604). Rejecting most of their suggestions, he willingly consented to one, a new translation of the Bible which we have come to call the Authorized King James Version. James wished to supplant the Geneva Bible used by the Puritans with his own version that would strengthen the authority of the king. As to the Puritans, he told them to conform or leave the country. By the summer of 1630 nearly a thousand Puritans had landed near Boston.

Among those fleeing England seeking greater religious freedom was Thomas Helwys. After some years in Holland he returned with members of his congregation to organize the first Baptist church in Britain. James had Helwys thrown into Newgate prison for his religious views where he soon died.

By the middle of the seventeenth century the conflict between king and Parliament reached its height. William Laud, the archbishop of Canterbury and an advisor to Charles I, took severe measures to suppress religious freedom. The Puritans fled England for the colonies. Those who remained rebelled.

A Civil War was fought pitting Parliament against the King. Parliament won, both Archbishop Laud and King Charles were beheaded, and the Commonwealth was formed. Parliament elected Oliver Cromwell to rule England. The Puritan led Parliament allowed a variety of churches to blossom. The people had a taste of religious freedom. When the commonwealth folded after the death of Cromwell, people sought religious freedom in the American colonies.

Today Christians in the United States have religious freedom guaranteed by our constitution. As you can see, it was a long time coming and the price was high, but a free society can not tolerate enforced religious conformity. Church and state must remain separate.

TRAVEL NOTES: WINCHESTER.

Pilgrimage is travel that transforms, travel to a specific site with the hope that what is experienced will change our lives. Pilgrims sought that experience of renewal by walking the Pilgrims' Way to Canterbury. The stories of pilgrims traveling from London to Becket's shrine in Canterbury is told in Chaucer's *Canterbury Tales.*

In Winchester we stayed at the Royal Hotel, a classy seventeenth century inn with an attractive walled garden within easy reach of the cathedral. This ancient cathedral city, founded by the Romans, was the capital of Britain under Alfred, a Saxon king, and then William, the Norman king.

Ancient walls surround an extensive lawn on which stands one of Britain's longest cathedrals (556 ft.). Started in 1079 and completed in 1093, Winchester cathedral with its twelve-bay nave is strikingly beautiful. Jane Austen is buried here.

The Pilgrims' Way begins at the west door of the cathedral. We followed it by car to Alton, one of the main halting places for pilgrims walking the well-worn route. Having served a pastorate in Alton, Illinois, I was delighted to drive through it.

Continuing to parallel the Pilgrims' Trail we drove on to Farnham and Guildford, then Dorking and Reigate. The high speed M roads moved us quickly past Maidstone and Leeds Castle to our destination, Canterbury.

TRAVEL NOTES: CANTERBURY.

Magnolia House, located just outside the city walls, was a welcome site. The lovely room on the first floor held a large poster bed, a view of a backyard garden filled with vines and flowers, and a sumptuous, modern bath. We dined at the Falstaff, a thirteenth century oak-paneled inn that proclaims its name from a sign hanging from beautiful wrought iron work.

The next morning we first walked to the church of St. Dunstan-Without-the-Westgate where Henry is said to have changed his clothes before walking humbly to visit the site where Beckett was martyred. From there we crossed the River Stour and went through the Westgate, the traditional pilgrim entrance to the city. We walked down crooked streets with their timber-framed houses jutting over the pavements as we went in search of the cathedral. We spent a leisurely day exploring the city, visiting first the cathedral, then the ruins of St. Augustine's Abbey, and finally, St. Martin's church, one of the oldest continually worshiping churches in England.

Entering the cathedral we traveled the same steps deeply worn by countless pilgrims to the place where Becket fell and then up the steps to Trinity chapel, the site of Becket's shrine before another Henry, the VIII, had it removed. Now only a mosaic and a single, large candle mark the site. The day drew to a close with evensong in the cathedral, cappuccino at The Monk's Tale, a coffee shop nearby, and, worn out by all the walking, a taxi home. As much as we could be, we were pilgrims.

REFLECTIONS: RELIGIOUS LIBERTY - Leviticus 25:10

"Proclaim LIBERTY throughout all the Land unto all the inhabitants thereof. Lev. XXV X"
Inscription on the Liberty Bell, Philadelphia

The Israelites were making a fresh start out in the desert. They had left Egypt behind and were forming a new nation freed from the oppression they had known. This statement was part of the rules they adopted to govern their life in the promised land.

This quote from Leviticus is found on the bell that was rung on July 8, 1776, from the tower of Independence Hall summoning citizens to hear the first public reading of the Declaration of Independence. The line in the Bible immediately preceding "proclaim liberty" is, "And ye shall hallow the fiftieth year." The 50th year is to be a year of Jubilee, a time of joy, a time for a fresh start. The bell had been ordered by the Pennsylvania Assembly in 1751 to commemorate the fiftieth anniversary of William Penn's Charter of Privileges (1701), its original Constitution. Penn was an advocate of religious freedom, Native American rights, and the inclusion of citizens in enacting laws. What better way could there be to honor Penn on that anniversary than with a bell proclaiming liberty?

Our Bill of Rights protects our religious liberty; it operates to protect us against the tyranny of the majority who may establish one way of religious practice for all. Religious liberty means religious organizations must be treated differently than secular organizations in order to protect that freedom.

Religious liberty also means that government, established by the majority, may not force those of differing faiths to participate in the practice of that faith. "Public school teachers can voice the Pledge of Allegiance, recite the Gettysburg Address and say a lot of other things in the class; but they may not lead in prayer or preside over religious exercises. Government may hang a picture of the president in public buildings or of George Washington in schools; but it ordinarily may not display a religious symbol or a portrait of Jesus. These limitations in religion operate to ensure government neutrality and promote religious liberty for all, especially for the minority. The majority in a democracy can sometimes be as tyrannical as a dictator in a totalitarian regime, especially with regard to religion."[3]

CLOSING

"Thanks be to thee, Lord Jesus Christ,
for all the benefits which thou hast won for us,
for all the pains and insults which thou has borne for us.
O merciful Redeemer, Friend and Brother,
may we know thee more clearly,
love thee more dearly, and
follow thee more nearly,
day by day."[4]

Credited with this prayer is Richard deWych (1197-1253), chancellor of Oxford, and, after his return from exile for his political views, bishop of Chichester.

PART TWO

PROFILES

"To be a Christian is to change,
to become new.
It is not simply a matter
of choosing a new life style . . . ,
it has to do with being a new person.
The new person
does not emerge full-blown.
Conversion,
passing from life to death
may be the miracle of a moment,
but the making of a saint
is the task of a lifetime."[1]

Maxie D. Dunnam

- 3 -

THOMAS HELWYS

An Inviting People

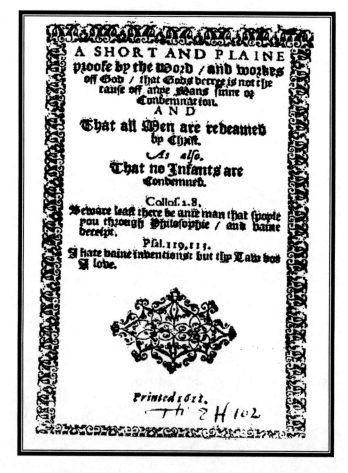

Flyleaf from A Short and Plain Proofe

Editions of his books from which this flyleaf was copied are found in the Duke Humphrey's Library in Oxford.

20

THOMAS HELWYS (c.1570 - c.1615)

Thomas Helwys, a lawyer by profession, was born of a prominent family of gentleman farmers in the Trent River Valley of Nottinghamshire, Britain. He studied law at prestigious Gray's Inn, the British legal society, and earned a comfortable living as a lawyer from 1592-1606. He married Joan Ashmore in 1595. Parliament passed an act with severe penalties that was to affect them both. Everyone had to conform to rules of the Church of England and worship only in its churches.

Around 1605 Helwys became a disciple in the Nonconformist (those who would not conform) congregation gathered at Gainsborough by John Smyth. The Helwys home at Broxtowe Hall soon became a haven for other Nonconformists. Within a year or two Helwys fled to Amsterdam to avoid persecution. There he helped plant a church with Smyth.

Helwys became the financial angel for the struggling congregation, assisting several others in fleeing persecution. In retaliation King James authorized the arrest of Helwys' wife, Joan, seized Broxtowe Hall along with all their other assets, and imprisoned Joan in 1608 in York Castle. By 1609 the attempt to renew the church through the study of God's word led the congregation to affirm that baptism should be for believers only upon confession of faith in Jesus. They also came to believe that Jesus died for us all, not just the elect, so that everyone should be extended an invitation to follow Jesus.

Smyth baptized the members of the congregation including Helwys, but not by immersion. He sought to merge the Nonconformist congregation with the Waterlander Mennonites, but before he could, he died of tuberculosis. A remnant under the leadership of Thomas Helwys and John Murton refused to become Mennonites, denied Smyth membership in the congregation, re-evaluated their original decision to leave England, and in 1611 returned the following year to organize the first Baptist congregation in Great Britain at Spitalfields, outside of London.

They believed that salvation was "generally" for anyone, as opposed to the Calvinists who believed only certain predesignated persons would be saved, so they became known as General Baptists. Evangelism became a way of life for them because, since everyone had the opportunity to be saved, everyone should hear the gospel. Using the Bible as their guidebook, rather than church tradition, during the Lord's Supper they broke the bread rather than cut it, and sat rather than knelt to eat it.

While in Amsterdam, Helwys and his supporters drew up a *Declaration of Faith of the English People Remaining at Amsterdam in Holland* (1611) in which they emphasized that God wishes us all to be saved. They believed that "the church of Christ is a company of faithful people . . . separated from the world by the Word and Spirit of God . . . being bound unto the Lord and unto one another by baptism . . . upon their own confession of the faith."[1] They stressed that although in Christ there is one Church, it consists of individual congregations, each of which, guided by the Bible, is immediately responsible to Christ alone. It was one of the earliest requests in England for total religious liberty available to everyone.

In his defense of not baptizing infants, Helwys wrote "*A Short and Plain Proof That No Infants Are Condemned.*" In it he attacks the Calvinists who would assign infants to hell if they died before they could assume responsibility for their sins.

After returning with his supporters to England Helwys wrote an appeal for religious liberty, *A Short Declaration of the Mistery of Iniquity,* (1612) which asked King James for toleration of both their beliefs and those of other non-conformists. In it he explained their conviction that it was their Christian duty not to flee from persecution. He made clear the congregation realized the possible consequences of their return, but they had come to lay down their lives in their own country for Christ and his truth.

King James' copy of the book, inscribed by Helwys to James, is found in the Duke Humphrey's Library in Oxford. James ignored Helwys' plea for toleration and in 1615 imprisoned him in Newgate Prison where he died soon afterwards. The congregation, led by John Murton, another returned exile, survived by going underground to avoid persecution.

TRAVEL NOTES: OXFORD

The original core library is named after Duke Humphrey, who by the time of his death in 1447 had presented several hundred books to the university. The library was moved in the 1480's to the second floor of the Divinity School Building. In order to protect these valuable books, they were chained to the reading desks. The original bookcases are dark, wooden shelves, placed back to back, extending perpendicularly from the walls in what is called the stall system. In the late sixteenth century Sir Thomas Bodley, a collector of medieval manuscripts, refurbished and restocked the university library. Today the Bodleian, the main library of Oxford, holds over six million volumes. The Duke Humphrey's library, now houses only ancient manuscripts.

Superintendent William Hodges welcomed us to the Duke's marvelous library and graciously allowed us to take the only elevator, a small cage for two, while he climbed the stairs. In a dark corner nook under the light of a desk lamp we held and examined the first editions of some of Thomas Helwys's books marveling at their condition. They are the size of a modern paperback with calfskin covers. The print had bled through many pages of the paper. We read the personal note signed by Thomas Helwys on the flyleaf inside the edition that he sent to King James. The books and the movement Thomas Helwys started, survived. This was the source of Baptist beginnings.

We contacted people by letter and e-mail when planning this pilgrimage. They were friendly, caring, and extremely helpful. The Duke Humphrey's Library is restricted to readers with special permission, permission we received by e-mail. Superintendent Hodges could not have been more gracious in welcoming us and allowing us to see and hold the books.

TRAVEL NOTES: REGENT'S PARK COLLEGE

Before leaving town we stopped briefly at Regent's Park College which was moved from Regent's Park, London to Oxford in 1927. The college, working with the Baptist Union of Great Britain, prepares men and women for the ordained Baptist ministry. The Angus Library, a special archive at the college, has an extensive collection of manuscripts from Nonconformist and Baptist heritages. We walked the grounds noting the names of famous Baptists, including Thomas Helwys, carved in stone.

CLOSING REFLECTIONS - Acts 8:26-31, 34-40

In *The Acts of the Apostles*, Luke writes that Philip responds to a request to know more about the Messiah. Knowing the gospel story, he relates what God has done through Jesus. At the close of his story, Philip invites the man to become a disciple of Jesus and to be baptized. The power of that moment sent the official down the road, rejoicing.

Thomas Helwys invited people to be part of the covenant community, "which covenant is, they which believe and are baptized shall be saved. The words whereof being spoken by him that made it, do with authority convince to the consciences of all that will hear them, that this covenant is made only with them that believe and are baptized."[2] We invite people to become disciples of Jesus so that they may mature in their faith and become, as did Philip, witnesses to it.

CLOSING

"Fare you well. Peace and love, with Faith. From God, and From our Lord Jesus Christ, be with all them that are in Christ Jesus. Amen."

Thomas Helwys."[3]

God Save ye Kinge

Spittlefeild n'eare Londone   *Tho: Helwys.*

Inscribed in his book to King James

HANSERD KNOLLYS

Tolerance on Trial

St. Catharine's College, Cambridge

HANSERD KNOLLYS (c.1599 - 1691)

Elizabeth I was nearing the end of her reign when Hanserd Knollys was born around 1599 in Cawkwell, a small town (three houses) in Lincolnshire on the east coast of England. Parish records indicate he was baptized eleven years later on November 13, 1609. The delay may have been because his father, a vicar with Puritan leanings, wanted him to be old enough to understand its meaning and make a personal commitment.

Knollys was educated at St. Catharine's College in Cambridge. He taught for a year at the Free School in Gainsborough, a center for Separatists. After his ordination in 1629 he was appointed to a small church at Humberstone, where three years later he married Anne Cheney on May 22, 1632. Racked with doubt about the direction of his ministry and having doubts about the practices of the state church, he resigned, despite the request of his bishop to continue in office.

Hanserd Knollys turned to John Wheelwright, a Separatist pastor, for advice. He told him to "to stop focusing so much on good works and to trust God's grace."[1] Because of his preaching, Wheelwright soon fled to New England. Knollys and his family were soon to follow him. Wheelwright had some success gathering a congregation in Braintree, near Boston, and then Quincy. He left there first for Exeter, New Hampshire and then Wells, Maine. In 1647 he returned to serve a church in Hampton, New Hampshire where he died in 1679.

Charles I became king when James I died in 1625, but unrest continued. Tension between the state church and the Separatists was high. Knollys found his calling to the ministry in Acts 26:16. "I have appeared to you to appoint you as my servant. You are to tell others what you have seen of me today and what I will show you in the future." He was arrested for nonconformist preaching in Boston, England. After witnessing to his jailer, he was allowed to escape to London where he hid for six weeks. Then on April 26, 1638, at age forty he and his wife and one or more of their children sailed for Boston, Massachusetts to seek religious freedom.

Knollys' radical reputation had preceded him. Gov. John Winthrop and John Cotton, head of First Church, tolerant only of those who did not disagree with them, denied him the right to preach or even teach. Banished from Massachusetts by the Puritans, he first went to Portsmouth, then to Dover, New Hampshire to preach.

Within the year after complaining that Massachusetts was more oppressive than England, Knollys was once again forced to move. In his letter of apology which the governor demanded, Knollys expressed his sorrow for the lack of tolerance. He had found intolerance, not only in London, but in the colonies. He resented it.

The family left for Long Island where, shortly afterwards, in response to a request by his elderly father and, after only three years in the colonies, he returned home with a pregnant wife and a three year old child.

By now England's political and religious climate had radically changed. When Civil War broke out in 1642, Oliver Cromwell called for volunteers for Parliament's army. Knollys enlisted as a chaplain in the Manchester division, while continuing to serve a church and to lecture. He resigned his commission when his commanders turned on Parliament and backed the Royalists.

John Milton, a friend of Knollys and of Roger Williams, wrote tracts in support of the Protestant cause. Milton was one of England's greatest poets, noted for the poem *Paradise Lost*.

At this point two distinct groups of Baptists were developing: the General Baptists, founded by Thomas Helwys, who believed salvation was "generally" for anyone who believed; and the Particular Baptists who believed salvation was only for the "elect," a belief held by most of the early Calvinist Puritans.

In 1644 Knollys was attracted to an Independent (Congregationalist) church led by John Spilsbury. "Membership was open to any who had been baptized, either as infants or as believers. Talented lay persons were allowed to share in the ministry, and the church voted that it would remain in harmony with other new churches that were forming. The tolerance of this early church was remarkable." [2]

A year later in 1645 Hanserd Knollys left to gather one of the first Particular Baptist congregations in London which he served for more than forty years. In 1646 he helped revise the London Baptist Confession of Faith of 1644 giving it more of a Calvinist orientation.

Gathered congregations did not have the support nor salaries of the state-mandated congregations, so clergy had to be "tent makers." Knollys taught school and worked for the government. Over the years the congregation, begun next to Great St. Helen's Church in London, moved to Swan Alley, Coleman Street, then George Yard in Whitechapel. At the time of his death in 1691, it was meeting at Broken Wharf, Thames Street in London.

By the end of the Civil War the power of the state church had been checked. Archbishop Laud along with Charles had been executed and the prayer book was banned. By 1654 Oliver Cromwell had become Lord Protector, declining the title of king with its right to succession. He eventually dismissed Parliament thus failing to lay a firm foundation for the commonwealth. When a movement developed to crown Cromwell king, Hanserd Knollys and eighteen other Baptists including John Clarke from Rhode Island petitioned him to not accept the title.

The years of the Commonwealth under Cromwell were harvest-time for the Baptists in England and Wales. They planted more than 130 churches. Shortly before Charles II returned, Knollys was accused of treason, a case of guilt by association with the Fifth Monarchists, and imprisoned in Newgate. Pardoned and released later that year, he went into self-exile for three years, first in Holland and then Germany with his wife and two children. From a distance he endorsed authors such as Benjamin Keach, author of a children's book, and Katherine Sutton, a writer of prayers and spiritual songs. In the debate over use of hymns in the church, he was clearly on the side of the singers. Charles II reestablished the state church, mandated the use of the prayer book once again, and penalized dissenters, including Roman Catholics, for teaching or preaching.

Returning to England, Knollys survived the Great Plague that terrorized London killing more than 68,000. He stayed with his congregation, All Hallows Church, unlike many who escaped to the country. Following the plague came the Great Fire destroying in five days more than 13,000 homes and almost 100 churches.

After his wife of forty years, Anne, died on April 30, 1671, he began writing a brief autobiography. Eight years later at the age of 81, he wrote a commentary on the Book of Revelation comparing Charles II to the "Beast" in John's Revelation.

The next king, James II, sought to reestablish Roman Catholicism. Knollys, now 84, refused to support James and so was thrown in jail. Parliament, fearing a return to Catholicism, offered the Crown to William III of Orange, a Dutch Protestant, and his wife, Mary, who was James's daughter. They were crowned jointly in Westminster Abbey in 1689. The Toleration Act and a Bill of Rights were passed later that year extending toleration to Trinitarian Protestants. Freedom of worship was granted to all, except Catholics or Unitarians, who would swear an oath of allegiance to the civil government.

On May 21, 1689 the General Baptists gathered to organize. Later that year the Particular Baptists, including Hanserd Knollys and Benjamin Keach, formed the first Particular Baptist association. Knollys died two years later on September 19, 1691 at the age of 93. Both he and his wife, Anne, are buried in Bunhill Fields, the only cemetery in England that would accept the bodies of free church members.

A few years later in 1696 John Farmer and his wife, friends of the Knollys, moved to Philadelphia where they joined the First Baptist Church. And so the Baptist family tree grew.

TRAVEL NOTES: CAMBRIDGE.

In 1627 Knollys entered St. Catharine's College at Cambridge, a center for Puritan theology, founded as Katherine Hall in 1473 for the study of theology and philosophy. Other records indicate he matriculated in 1629 at the Easter term.

Although the college was closed to visitors because of spring exams, we had been given advance permission to wander around the campus. The courtyard is reminiscent of a monastic setting with buildings forming a quadrangle. The flowers were colorful and delightfully varied.

Virtually nothing is left that predates Knollys days on the campus. The oldest part, the main court, dates from the end of the seventeenth century. The chapel was built between 1694 and 1704.

REFLECTIONS ON TOLERATION - Acts 26: 12-16

Hanserd Knollys found his calling in this text. This final defense by Paul of his calling combines themes from the past. Paul begins with a claim to Jewish loyalty, repeats his conversion with special emphasis on his commission, and concludes with an assertion of his obedience. Paul believed he received his commission directly from Jesus.

Hanserd Knollys was inspired by this passage to tell others what he had seen and would see of Jesus. He stood for toleration in a time when people were intolerant.

Intolerance is a danger even now. Our Bill of Rights protects minorities from the wishes of the majority. Religions are to be treated equally under the law and religious liberty is to be granted to all, especially minorities. We are free to believe as we choose and to act according to our own consciences, as long as we do not interfere with the freedom of others.

We may be called to invite others to believe as we do, to call them to follow Jesus, but we must do this through love rather than force, reaching out in caring witness rather than penalizing those who do not believe as we do. Thus we are called to be tolerant of those who do not believe as we do.

Some believe tolerance means indifference or the absence of values. Actually, it means allowing others the freedom to believe and freely witness to what they believe. Their witness may differ from ours, yet we may come together to determine the common ground we share, the common ground on which we are able to build a ministry.

CLOSING

"And now my dearly beloved Brethern and Sisters, I commit you all to the Word of his Grace, which is able to build you up, and to give you an Inheritance among them which are Sanctified. So I remain, while in this Tabernacle. Hanserd Knollys."[3]

With this blessing Hanserd Knollys closed the last letter he wrote to his congregation.

- 5 -

ROGER WILLIAMS

Peace and Justice

The Old Chapel, Pembroke College, Cambridge, England

ROGER WILLIAMS (1603-83)

James I was on the throne when Roger Williams was born in Cow Lane in London to Alice and James Williams, a member of the Merchant Tailor Company. Williams was raised an Anglican.

Sir Edward Coke, a wealthy and successful lawyer who was chief justice of the Court of Common Pleas, asked Roger Williams who was still in his teens to record court trials for him via shorthand. It was here in court Williams learned about laws and contracts.

Coke was an advocate of freedom of speech. He sponsored Williams at Charterhouse Grammar School and later at Pembroke College, Cambridge (1624-7). While at Cambridge Williams came into contact with Puritans, who believed that the only way to "purify" the church was to separate it from government control. After a frustrating two years working on his Masters degree in theology, he left to become a chaplain at Oates in Essex, the home of Sir William Masham, a leader in the Puritan movement. During his time there he met Oliver Cromwell and Thomas Hooker, a nonconformist, who later founded Hartford, Connecticut. On December 15, 1629, Williams married Mary Barnard, daughter of a Puritan clergyman.

When Charles I became king, Archbishop Laud began a ruthless persecution of those who would not conform to the state church, driving the Puritans who wished to purify the churches from within to seek asylum first in Holland and then in Massachusetts. In December 1630 in Bristol, hoping to be part of that purer church, Roger and Mary Williams boarded a ship, the Lyon, for New England. Young and handsome, well-educated and an able preacher, he was welcomed in the colony and offered a teaching position in the Boston church. He refused the call because the church would not completely separate from the state churches. He criticized the local government for forcing persons to conform to religious laws governing the Sabbath. His stay in Boston was stormy and brief, but it left a lasting impression.

Salem invited him to be their parish teacher. The Salem church had adopted this simple, open-ended covenant, "We Covenant with the Lord and one with another, and do bind ourselves in the presence of God, to walk together in all his ways, according as he is pleased to reveal himself unto us in his Blessed word of truth." Since both Roger and Mary could affirm this covenant, they joined in 1631. When he was invited to assist the Salem parish minister and fellow Cambridge graduate, Samuel Skelton, Boston objected and Salem withdrew the offer.

Roger and Mary headed south still seeking religious freedom. The Pilgrims, unlike the Puritans, had separated from the Church of England. There Williams assisted Ralph Smith, a pastor, and began his long ministry with the Native Americans. In 1633 Mary gave birth to their first child. They supplemented their meager income by farming and trading with the Narragansetts, Wampanoags, and Neponsets.

Although more tolerant than the Puritans, the Pilgrims also reserved the right to determine the religious beliefs of their colonists. Within a year, dissatisfied once more, Roger and Mary headed back to Salem where the church made him an elder, teacher, and, when Samuel Skelton became ill and eventually died, pastor. There Williams called the congregation to separate politics and religion, and not to force conversion, especially for the Native Americans. Land was to be negotiated for rather than taken by decree from the Native Americans. Justice was not served by a state church because, by definition, it was a political church; Christendom was not Christianity! Requiring a person to swear an oath ending with "so help me God" if that person didn't believe in God was questioned. The Salem church, which continued to support him, was not willing to separate from the other churches, so he resigned.

Although the Boston court gave him six weeks to pack up and leave the Massachusetts jurisdiction, it allowed him to stay in Salem under order not to preach until he left. But Mary continued with the church and Roger held meetings in their home, so the court sent a ship to deport him back to England. Warned by friends and believing he had a better chance for survival with his Native American friends than in England, they fled three days before the ship arrived.

When spring came, Canonicus, chief of the Narragansetts, granted him some land. He had befriended the Narragansetts in the past; they cared for him now. In June 1636 after being in New England for five years, Roger and Mary Williams had finally found a home. Building a house near a large pool of fresh spring water on a wooded hill overlooking the Salt River, they, along with their friends from Salem, created Providence Plantation just outside of the Bay jurisdiction. Under Williams' leadership, the community became the first modern government from which power over religious practice was eliminated. Separation of church and state and liberty of conscience were proclaimed and practiced there.

The area attracted persons who sought freedom to worship as they wished. When expelled from Boston for her religious views, Anne Hutchinson, probably the first woman to gather a congregation in America, moved with her followers to what is now Portsmouth. A year later Newport, where John Clarke was both physician and pastor, was founded. Warwick became the fourth village in what was to eventually become the colony of Rhode Island.

Williams began gathering friends and family in his home for worship. Among them were Richard and Catherine Scott, a sister of Anne Hutchinson. The Scotts may have been Baptists in Britain. After becoming part of Williams' congregation, Catherine convinced Roger that baptism of believers, not infant baptism, was the way of scripture. Governor Winthrop wrote in his journal that sometime before March 1639, Williams, since no Baptist pastor had arrived from England, was baptized by Ezekiel Holliman, a member of the church at Salem. The congregation organized around the principle of congregational polity (no outside authority could tell them what to do), affirmed baptism of believers (but not yet by immersion), and advocated separation of church and state. Richard Scott who later became a Quaker wrote, "I walked with him in the Baptist way about four months, in which time he broke with his society and declared at large the ground and reason for it."[1] Williams, disenchanted with all churches, became a Seeker. He never again formally affiliated with a congregation.

Williams left for London in 1643 to secure a charter for his colony and a printer for his books. His book about Native Americans, *A Key into the Language of America*, was a success in England, opening important doors in his quest for a charter for the colony. After being granted the charter by Charles I, Williams moved on to the issue of religious freedom, labeling what was happening as "spiritual rape." One reign commanded worship one way, the next another. Since there was no religious freedom, those who were out of favor were persecuted. In mid-July of 1644 his, *The Bloudy Tenent of Persecution, for cause of Conscience* was published. Although it fueled a book burning in London, Roger Williams was already on his way home with enough copies to prevent its being lost.

Even though Williams left the church he had served in Providence and sought no other, he continued to defend Baptists in their struggle for religious freedom when Massachusetts outlawed them in 1644. Williams wrote in 1649 that Baptists were requiring baptism by immersion. It had been introduced by English Baptists to John Clarke's Newport church in 1648 who then had passed it on to Providence where it spread north to Rehoboth. The Puritans in Massachusetts were ruthless in trying to control how others worshiped. Baptists were jailed and beaten for preaching and four Quakers were hanged in Boston for their beliefs.

When their charter was threatened, Roger Williams and John Clarke sailed for England in 1651 to appeal to Parliament. The Council of State encouraged the four towns to continue as they were, but the charter remained in question. Williams' relationship with Oliver Cromwell and John Milton gave him access to influential people. Three years later Williams left for home leaving John Clarke behind in London to finish the task of obtaining a charter for the colony. On July 8, 1663, Charles II granted the "poor colony" a royal charter.

By November Williams had been elected governor of the colony (1654-57). As chief officer of the new colony, Williams wrestled with how to implement religious freedom and bring peace and justice in decisions of church and state.

The bloody King Philip's War (1675-6) between colonists and the native tribes destroyed most of his resources. Roger Williams died in 1683.

Rhode Island under Williams became a haven for religious liberty. Baptists flowed there only to divide as they had done in England into General and Particular Baptists. Then a group of Seventh Day Baptists formed. Roger Williams had created the climate in which religious freedom, and as a result, Baptists, could survive and find new freedom in a new land.

TRAVEL NOTES: HOPEWELL, NEW JERSEY

In 1715 the Stout family helped form a Baptist church in Hopewell, New Jersey. By 1747 a sanctuary was built on land given them by Jonathan Hart, the only Baptist to sign the Declaration of Independence. The lovely brick church is still there on Main Street surrounded by the cemetery in which stands a monument to Hart. Isaac Eaton became their pastor and the Hopewell Academy was founded in his home just down the street. A member of the church, John Gano, went on to serve as pastor of the First Baptist Church of New York (1762-87). During the war years he was a chaplain in the army (1776-81) serving with Washington at the critical battles of Princeton, Morristown, and Yorktown.

The Hopewell congregation grew to more than 600 members at its peak only to gradually decline and die when it refused to adopt new ways of ministry. It became an Old School Baptist Church and refused to participate in the Sunday School or Mission movements of the nineteenth century. The last member died shortly after we led a service in its sanctuary celebrating the 200th anniversary of the Declaration of Independence.

TRAVEL NOTES: CAMBRIDGE.

The streets are narrow and often one way in Cambridge, a college town on the banks of the River Cam. At Pembroke, founded in 1347 by the wife of the Earl of Pembroke, we were warmly welcomed by Nick Baskey, the bursar, and Judy Pullen Squire, his personal assistant. The college is close to St. Catharine's College where Hanserd Knollys attended. The librarian prepared a packet of materials for us on Roger Williams giving us a British view of this unique American.

For more than 300 years the college occupied buildings in one small, square court, now First Court. Its chapel, the first at Cambridge (1366), became the Old Library when a new chapel was finished in 1665, the first work of Christopher Wren. The chapel was an expression of gratitude by Wren's uncle, the Bishop of Ely, after the Restoration. The gardens are extensive and lovely. Gideon, who often leads tours of the lovely, old campus, escorted us around the quadrangle. Although the dorm room where it is believed Roger Williams lived from 1623-27 was demolished in a renovation project, many of the original buildings remain. Francis Mundy, a Fellow of the College in 1714 wrote in his farewell letter that it was his wish "That Learning, good Humour, and pleasant Conversation may flourish at Pembroke Hall."[2] We were reassured that it still does.

TRAVEL NOTES: PROVIDENCE, RHODE ISLAND

James Manning, a graduate of Isaac Eaton's Academy in Hopewell in 1758 and later of Princeton College in 1762, was called in 1764 to found a Baptist college in Rhode Island. Manning became the pastor of the First Baptist Church in Providence and under his leadership in 1774-5 their striking sanctuary, now restored to its original appearance, was built. The college became Brown University.

We visited Providence in the spring. The city has created a beautiful park in which stands a statue of Williams overlooking the city. Nearby is the sanctuary of the First Baptist Church, an impressive New England colonial style building that holds 1,400. The design, highly influenced by the New England meeting house style, is square, lacks religious symbols, and places the pulpit in the center emphasizing the preaching of the Word. The steeple, the first on a Baptist church in New England, is a copy of one proposed for St. Martin's-in-the- Fields in London. There is a self-guided tour of the building. A few artifacts of Roger Williams are on display.

The First Baptist Church of Providence, Rhode Island

REFLECTIONS ON JUSTICE - Amos 5:18-24

Amos had very pointed messages to the rich and powerful, especially those who pretended to be deeply religious but were oppressing others. Amos was a sensitive man, angered by the cruel treatment of people in his society, and moved to speak out in a powerful way much as Roger Williams did in his day.

Within our churches and our country there is a renewed commitment to justice issues. The fight against injustice is a tough one, often involving conflict. We contribute to injustice by our quiet acquiescence. Pick your issue and become involved. Let the world know you care! Justice is our unfinished business.

CLOSING

Roger Williams graciously allowed others freedom of conscience as much as he sought it for himself. May we also allow others the freedom we seek.

"I desire not that liberty to myself which I would not freely and impartially weight out to all the consciences of the world besides; therefore, I humbly conceive that it is the express and absolute duty of the civil powers to proclaim an absolute freedom of conscience in all the world."[3]

JOHN CLARKE

A Lively Experiment

A stone marker in Newport, Rhode Island

JOHN CLARKE (1609-76)

John Clarke, a theologian and a physician, emigrated to New England in 1637 seeking religious freedom. Not finding it in Boston, he settled in Newport where he gathered a congregation which is probably the first Baptist congregation in America to practice baptism of believers by immersion.

John Clarke was born in Westhorpe, Suffolk County, England on October 3, 1609, to Thomas and Rose Kerrich Clarke and baptized in the local church within the week. They had eight children, five of whom eventually joined John in New England.

Although Clarke was well educated, we are uncertain where. There is a strong possibility that he attended the Bury St. Edmunds school near Westhorpe. The records at St. Catharine's College in Cambridge where Hanserd Knollys had been educated, show a John Clarke beginning his studies during the Easter term, 1627 and then receiving a B.A. in 1630-31.

Clarke studied medicine, probably at the University of Leyden in Holland where he would have rubbed shoulders with radical Christians including Baptists. While in London seeking a charter for Rhode Island, he worked as a legal counselor at Gray's Inn and also published a Biblical concordance. John Clarke became an expert physician, a recognized legal advocate, a wise theologian, and an astute politician; he was, like Thomas Jefferson, truly a renaissance man.

Dr. John and Elizabeth Harges Clarke arrived in Boston in November 1637 just a year after Roger Williams had been exiled from there. With a winning personality, a stature of six feet, well educated, and happily married, he was ready to make his mark on the world in this new country.

The Clarkes had left England seeking freedom of religious expression. Not finding it in the established church in Boston, they joined with others who sought sanctuary beyond the reach of either the Massachusetts or Plymouth Bay colonies. The Narragansetts, influenced by Williams, on March 24, 1638, granted land on Aquidneck Island (Isle of Peace) in Narragansett Bay where Portsmouth, a community free from religious restrictions, was founded. Within the year Clarke and others relocated to the southern tip of the island, where they established the village of Newport. There they adopted a democratic form of government with laws agreed upon by a majority of the freemen (property-owning persons). They named the colony Rhode Island after the Greek Isle of Rhodes and adopted as its official seal a sheaf of arrows bound together marked with the motto "Amor Vincet Omnia" (Love Conquers All).

About this time Roger Williams headed for England to officially charter Providence Plantation. He returned with a contract that merged the towns of Portsmouth, Newport, Providence and Warwick under the name of The Colony of the Providence Plantations in the Narragansett Bay in New England, omitting any reference to Rhode Island. Three years later the towns reluctantly accepted the charter. Clarke drew up a Law Code which was adopted in 1647.

We are not sure when John Clarke became a Baptist; some contend he may have been baptized at Elder Stillwell's church in London before he left England or that he became a Baptist while studying in Holland. That would explain his quiet but passionate pilgrimage to find a place free from persecution to practice the freedom he had found in Jesus.

Wherever Clarke went, he gathered a group to study the Bible and worship. In 1638 he helped organize an independent church in Portsmouth which included a number of Baptists. Later he withdrew to gather a congregation in Newport. Because the records are unclear, we will never know if John Clarke or Roger Williams was the first to organize a church that regularly baptized its members. Gov. Winthrop recorded that Roger Williams and members of his congregation were baptized in 1639. Williams later concluded that his baptism was invalid and left the church. Although the Newport congregation had been taking shape since March 1638, the records indicate by 1648 it had officially organized.

Baptism of believers by immersion rather than pouring soon followed. In 1648 Mark Lucar, a Particular Baptist pastor from England, settled at Newport where he shared with the congregation the views of the London Baptists including baptism by immersion. It soon became the norm in Baptist congregations.

In 1653 Lucar and Clarke led a crusade in Seekonk, Massachusetts where the record shows several converts upon profession of faith, were baptized by immersion. Roger Williams wrote of the event that John Clarke had baptized the converts by dipping, "a practice that comes nearer the first practice of our great Founder Christ Jesus; than other practices of religion do."[1] The Newport congregation was reaching out, taking the gospel to those who do not believe much as the British Baptists had.

The differences experienced in Britain influenced the Baptists in the colonies. When the Particular Baptists gained control of the Newport Baptist church, several General Baptist members left to form the Second Baptist Church of Newport in 1654. Other Baptist churches were also being formed. John Myles emigrated from Wales with a few of his members to charter a church in Massachusetts, the First Baptist Church of Swansea (1663). First Baptist Church of Boston (1665) was established soon afterwards. Correspondence flowed among the four churches as they sought each others support. The Newport church continued to assume a central role in organizing Baptist churches in America.

On a summer weekend Dr. John Clarke, Obadiah Holmes and John Crandall walked for three days to reach Lynn, Massachusetts to bring spiritual comfort to an older blind Baptist, William Witter. On Sunday, July 20, 1651, a few of the villagers quietly defied the law forbidding worship in any other manner than that dictated by the state and in peaceful resistance gathered two miles outside of town in Witter's home to hear Clarke preach. This tall, bearded, rather slender middle aged man held his audience with the fire of his convictions. Suddenly, town officials invaded the peaceful home, arresting the three. They were taken against their will to a Puritan religious meeting where Clarke boldly objected to their forced attendance, since this was not really a church because they practiced infant baptism. Two days later they were transported to Boston, imprisoned, and charged with denying the validity of one of the sacraments of the established church in Massachusetts, infant baptism, and of "rebaptizing" adults. Clarke objected to the phrase "re-baptizing" stating, "I have baptized many, but I never re-baptized any." Clarke was fined twenty pounds, Crandall five, and Holmes thirty, or "else be well whipped." When Holmes confessed, "I bless God I am counted worthy to suffer for the name of Jesus," Wilson, pastor of First Church Boston, cursed and struck him. Although all three refused to pay their fines, friends paid them. Holmes refused to accept the payment and the authorities were delighted to whip him. When the savage punishment ended, Holmes told them, "You have struck me as with roses." They had created not an example, but a martyr.

Holmes, an Oxford graduate, became pastor of the Newport congregation during the years Clarke was in England. He often related the story and showed the scars of his encounter with the state church. His descendants married into the Lincoln family. Abraham Lincoln's father, Thomas Lincoln, helped plant the Pigeon Creek Baptist Church in Indiana and served as its church moderator. It would be nice to think that Holmes influenced Lincoln's stand on liberty and freedom of conscience.

Clarke repeatedly requested a debate with the leading advocates of Puritanism but, fearing a wider hearing of his convincing arguments, they refused. He had four proposals for debate that are summarized here:

1. Jesus Christ is Lord and Savior and we are called to be his disciples;
2. baptism of believers by immersion is the only valid form;

3. every believer is to be allowed to speak in Church without fear of punishment; and

4. a believer's conscience should not be restricted by force.

Henry Dunster was so moved by the flogging of Holmes and the witness of Clarke that he professed Baptist views risking his presidency of Harvard.

While New England was acting like old England by persecuting those with differing religious views, old England was undergoing reform. Oliver Cromwell became head of the Commonwealth. Taking advantage of the changing climate, William Coddington sailed for England to apply for a charter for Rhode Island naming himself as governor for life. The colony sent John Clarke and Roger Williams in 1651 to ask that Coddington's charter be revoked. Mission accomplished, Williams headed for home while Clarke remained to represent the colony in seeking a new charter. While in England, Clarke joined a Particular Baptist Church led by William Kiffin. He published *"Ill Newes from New-England or a Narrative of New England's Persecutions (1652),"* a defense of religious freedom and of believers' baptism by immersion, plus a vivid description of the persecution of Baptists in Boston in 1651. In it he wrote how "Old England was becoming new (under Cromwell) and New England was becoming old (with its persecutions)." He also published *"A Concordance of the Bible (1655)."*

After Cromwell died, Clarke applied once again for a charter for the colony, this time securing the signature and seal of King Charles II on July 8, 1663, chartering it as "The Colony of Rhode Island and Providence Plantations." This charter granted religious freedom to a greater extent than had ever been given by an English king. For the first time a government would guarantee religious freedom.

The charter was so well written it remained in force until 1843 when Rhode Island adopted its present constitution. It is one of the resources Thomas Jefferson used in writing the Declaration of Independence. The following quote from the charter written by Dr. John Clarke is inscribed on the great marble dome on the Capitol building in Providence, Rhode Island: "That it is much on their hearts (if they may be permitted) to hold forth **a lively experiment,** that a most flourishing civil state may stand and best be maintained, and that among our English subjects, with a full liberty in religious concernments."[2]

Upon his return to Newport, Dr. Clarke resumed his medical practice, his ministry, and served as deputy governor of the colony. Clarke married three times; first to Elizabeth Harges, then Jane Fletcher in 1671, and finally a widow, Sarah Davis. Jane died shortly after giving birth to their only child, a daughter, who also died the next year. Clarke died on April 20, 1676 and is buried in Newport between Elizabeth and Jane. His ministry continues today through a trust fund, possibly the oldest active trust in this country, which he requested be used for the relief of the poor and the education of children. His life was "a lively experiment."

PILGRIM TRAVELS: NEWPORT

We traveled to Newport to visit the United Baptist (John Clarke Memorial) Church. In 1846 the current sanctuary was constructed on the site of a previous meeting house that had been built in 1738. Paul Hanson, its pastor, warmly welcomed us and graciously showed us the sanctuary and the historical displays. The congregation's roots lie in the church John Clarke gathered on the island in 1638.

The sanctuary is colonial in design with a balcony and private pews each with a door. A colonial clock hangs above the front entrance ticking with a regular beat. The historical rooms contain memorabilia and portraits of significant leaders in the congregation including one believed to be John Clarke.

In 1656 several members withdrew to form Second Baptist Church. Almost 200 years later in 1847 sixty members withdrew from Second Baptist to form Central Baptist Church. They were reunited sixty years later and by 1946 they had all become one congregation again, uniting under the name the United Baptist (John Clarke Memorial) Church.

The Gothic church built by Second Baptist Church in 1835 was torn down when the two congregations reunited. The church moved to the old Second Congregational building, which is now an apartment house. The original bell, cast in 1885 by the Jones Troy Foundry, is inscribed "First Baptist Church, Newport, R.I. Founded 1638 by Dr. John Clarke. The oldest Baptist Church in America." When it came down in the hurricane of 1938, it was donated to Camp Canonicus in Exeter, the Baptist camp in Rhode Island, where it still rings a joyful peal. The current tower bell is from the old Central Baptist Church.

From the church we drove a short distance to where Dr. Clarke, his first two wives, and several other people are buried. The site is owned by United Baptist Church and maintained by the Clarke Foundation. The inscription on his gravestone, erected in March 1840, reads:

"To the memory of Dr. John Clarke . . . one of the original purchasers and proprietors of the island and one of the founders of the First Baptist Church in Newport, its first pastor, and munificent benefactor. He was a native of Bedfordshire, England, and a practitioner of physics in London. He with his associates came to this island from Massachusetts in March, 1638 O.S. and on the 24th of the same month obtained a deed of it from the Indians. He shortly after gathered the church aforesaid, and became its pastor. . . . Mr. Clarke and Mr. Williams, two fathers of the colony strenuously and fearlessly maintained that none but Jesus Christ had authority over the conscience. He died April 20, 1676, in the 66th year of his age, and is there interred."

REFLECTIONS ON BAPTISM - Mark 1:5-11

Dr. John Clarke was an enthusiastic advocate of baptism of believers by immersion. In his book, *Ill Newes from New-England*, he cites several biblical reasons why "dipping" was the only acceptable form of baptism.

Mark 1:8 is usually translated "I baptized you with water," but the Greek word could also be translated "in" as the footnote in several translations notes. Clarke argued that Jesus was baptized "in water" not "with water."

Baptism as practiced by John was a dipping, washing of the whole body, symbolizing a cleansing of self from the life that had been lived.

The root meaning of the word "baptize" means to dip or immerse. Clarke cited the story of Naaman in 2 Kings 5:14 where "he went down and immersed himself seven times in the Jordan." He also referred to Acts 8 and the story of Philip and the Ethiopian official.

Clarke recognized baptism as a command of Jesus as cited in the Great Commission, "Go therefore and make disciples of all nations, baptizing them in the name of the Father and of the Son and of the Holy Spirit" (Matthew 28:19), and in several other New Testament references.

Louis Asher, a Clarke biographer, writes, "Clarke believed that the act of baptism requires a three-fold prerequisite: a proper subject, a believer; a proper design, immersion in water following a profession of faith in Christ; and a proper administrator, a duly baptized, divinely called, and spirit-led disciple who stands in the faithful exercise of the ministerial office - properly ordained and appointed. In baptism Clarke likened the act to a 'dying, or as it were a drowning, to hold forth death, burial and resurrection . . . . into the name of the Father, Son, and Holy Spirit."[3]

When we find new life in Jesus, what are we to do? Peter tells us at the close of his sermon, "Repent (turn back to God), and be baptized!" (Acts 2:38) They were and we still do baptize. Baptism marks our entrance as members into the universal Christian church.

Baptists have affirmed that as Jesus commands, only believers in Jesus as Lord and Savior may be baptized, and that by immersion. Jesus was immersed in the Jordan by John. One reason may have been to identify with those he came to save. When we are baptized as was he, we become part of that community that stretches back in time to Jesus and reaches today to the ends of the earth.

CLOSING PRAYER

Living God, you enter our hearts with your spirit and give us the power not only to survive but also to conquer the challenges that come our way. When justice burns like a flaming fire within us, when love evokes willing sacrifice from us, when we proclaim our belief in you, we know we have been empowered to fulfill the tasks you have given us. Comfort us, empower us, and prod us into doing what is good, and right, and just. Amen.

The record book, including the covenant, of the Swansea Baptist Churches John Myles, pastor

HENRY DUNSTER

The Love of Learning

**Chapel window at Magdalen College
Cambridge, England**

HENRY DUNSTER (1609-58)

Henry Dunster was born near Bury, England in 1609. During the 1627 Easter term he began his studies at Magdalene (pronounced Maud-lin), a college in Cambridge, England, completing them seven years later. Attending Cambridge at the time were John Milton and John Harvard. Dunster stayed on to teach for six years at Magdalene College.

Although he was ordained as an Anglican minister, he expressed some dissatisfaction with King Charles, the established church, and the Presbyterians. Deciding to leave for New England with his brother Richard, he said, "The sun shines as pleasantly on America as on England, and the Sun of Righteousness much more clearly." His sisters, Elizabeth, Mary, and Rose eventually joined the two brothers.

In 1636 when the Massachusetts Bay colonists voted to establish a college in New Town, they changed the name of the town to Cambridge in honor of the college from which some had graduated. A goal of four hundred pounds was set for buildings and equipment. It wasn't until John Harvard died and left them £850 and 400 books that the project received renewed interest and, with additional small gifts of money and land, work was begun on the college which now was to be named after Harvard.

Shortly after arriving in Boston in 1640, Henry Dunster was asked to head the college. Boston, a small village of 20-30 homes at the time, had only one lawyer, who, after three years, returned home because of lack of business. Dunster joined the Puritan Church in Cambridge and, when the pastor died in 1649, he served as interim.

Henry Dunster took the title of President, a Cambridge term for Vice-Master, since the post of Master, it is thought, had been intended for the Moravian scholar, Comenius. The use of the term "president" as the head of a college may have set the precedent for its use in other colleges and in the government we eventually formed.

As the first president of Harvard College, he labored for twelve years to create a college based on his Cambridge experiences. "The youngest in the long line of Harvard presidents, he proved to be one of the greatest."[1] He drew up a charter which imposed no religious tests. He recruited students and established fellowships. He taught Latin, Greek, and Hebrew and advocated education for the natives, starting a second college for them, thus making it truly a university.

During its early years he went unpaid as the college struggled financially. From his own valuable lands he gave the college more than 100 acres. There he built a president's home. Nine students graduated after the first two years.

Jesse and Elizabeth Glover had sailed with Dunster for Boston, bringing a printing press with them. When Jesse died, Dunster married Elizabeth, thus becoming guardian of their five children and the printing press. After revising the (Massachusetts) *Bay Psalm Book*, he printed copies of it. When his first wife died, he married Elizabeth Atkinson, and they had five children, three sons and two daughters.

So moved by the vicious beating of Obadiah Holmes and the arguments that Clarke made in defense of his faith, Dunster restudied the scriptures and what John Clarke had written about baptism of believers by immersion. He concluded that infant baptism was "unscriptural" and that following the primitive church practice, only adult believers should be baptized.

When his third child was born, Dunster refused to have her baptized. Although always an advocate of baptism by immersion, he now was committed to baptism of believers only and witnessed to it within his congregation. As a result in February 1654 he was called before a special conference of Boston clergy to defend his view that visible believers only should be baptized. Sincere efforts to change his mind failed. His example led others to reexamine their convictions and to follow in his footsteps. One of them, a good friend, Thomas Gould of Charlestown, eventually became the first pastor of the Baptist church in Boston when it was organized.

Finally church and state rose up to silence Henry Dunster. The General Court tried and convicted him of being "unsound in the faith" and instructed the overseers of the college to remove him. He was forced to resign his presidency and to move from the college he had created and from the house he had built. Reluctant to have him leave, the trustees told him he would be allowed to remain if he kept silent on the subject of baptism. Realizing he must speak what he believed, fourteen years after accepting the position of president, he left Harvard. The authorities at first were not willing to allow his family to remain for the remainder of the winter in the home he had built. Because of the illness of his wife and child, the demand was reversed on appeal so he and his family stayed until March.

When asked to profess something different from what he believed, he said, "I conceived then, and so do still, that I spake the truth in the fear of God, and dare not deny the same or go from it until the Lord otherwise teaches me; and this I pray the Honored Court to take for mine Answer."

The family first moved to Thomas Gould's home. Dunster was offered an opportunity to go to Dublin, Ireland to teach and minister there, but he quietly retired to Scituate in Plymouth Colony thus avoiding banishment from Boston. Scituate tolerated his Baptist views. He was active in a church there until he died on February 27, 1659. He is buried at First Church, Cambridge, where the college erected a memorial to him almost two hundred years later in 1846. Elizabeth survived him by thirty years.

President Chauncy, who succeeded Dunster, and Jonathan Mitchell, a pastor who opposed him, were graciously allowed to keep the books they had borrowed from him. The rest of his estate was left to his wife and two sons, Jonathan and David.

"To him Harvard owes . . . perhaps her very existence; for the college might have followed her first patron to an early death and oblivion but for the faith, courage, and intelligence of Henry Dunster."[2]

TRAVEL NOTES: CAMBRIDGE, ENGLAND

After visiting both Pembroke and St. Catharine in Cambridge, Judy and I drove north to Magdalene. Just as Henry Dunster would have done so many years before, we walked through the gateway built around 1585 into the First Court where he would have lived and studied. The bursar cordially welcomed us and, even though it was exam time, allowed us to wander, searching for signs of Dunster. We spotted a door dedicated to his memory by Harvard alumni and a stained glass window in the chapel that were a tribute to Dunster, Samuel Pepys, and Thomas Cranmer.

Originally Buckingham College and administered by the Benedictines, Magdalene was renamed after King Henry dissolved the monastic orders. By the seventeenth century the college had become a center of the Puritan movement, sending several of its members to settle in New England, among them Henry Dunster.

TRAVEL NOTES: SOUTHWARK, LONDON

After worshiping at the Metropolitan Tabernacle our first Sunday morning in London, we visited Southwark Cathedral, the second oldest Gothic church in London. A chapel in the cathedral is named for John Harvard who was baptized there in 1608. The American window features a scallop shell, the familiar sign of the pilgrim. There are memorials in the cathedral to William Shakespeare and to Sam Wannamaker, the American who helped restore the nearby Globe Theater.

REFLECTIONS - THE LOVE OF LEARNING (Psalm 1)

Henry Dunster had a love of learning and a respect for God that is "the beginning of wisdom." One of the first books he translated and printed was the Psalms. Here is Psalm 1 as translated by Henry Dunster for the Massachusetts Bay Psalm Book.[3]

Psalm One

1. O Blessed man that walks not in the advice of wicked men,
Nor standeth in the sinners way, nor scorners seat sits in.

2. But he upon Jehovah's law doth set his whole delight,
And in his law doth meditate both in the day and night.

3. He shall be like a planted tree by water brooks which shall
In his due season yield his fruit, whose leaf shall never fall:

4. And all he doth shall prosper well: the wicked are not so:
But they are like unto the chaff which wind drives to and fro.

5. Therefore shall not ungodly men in judgment stand upright:
Nor in the assembly of the just shall stand the sinful wight.

6. For of the righteous men, the Lord acknowledgeth the way:
Whereas the way of wicked men shall uttterly decay.

In this first Psalm which is an introduction to the other Psalms, the poet promises us we will also be blessed with wisdom when we turn from our wicked ways to meditating regularly on the word of God. When we are grounded in the scriptures, we will find meaning and purpose for our daily living.

The psalmist pictures a tree standing strong and erect in the face of wind and changing weather. Its roots draw life from the stream that flows by it; it produces fruit in its season. Happiness and joy are not rewards, but the results of a life lived within the guidelines of God. When we meditate on the scriptures and discuss how they relate to our lives with our friends, we will be encouraged to live by the basic principles we find there.

The psalmist goes on to contrast the lives of those who love God and walk in the Way with those who do not. They are like chaff which the wind scatters. Back in Biblical days when grain was harvested it was laid on the threshing floor and crushed, breaking open the ears of grain. The chaff, the empty husks and the crushed straw, were then separated from the grain by tossing them into the air. The wind would blow the chaff away, while the heavier grain would fall, be gathered, and ground into flour. The psalmist implies that those who do not obey the Lord are easily blown about by the shifting ways of opinion since they have nothing to guide their lives.

The psalmist concludes that those who choose to follow the way of God will be blessed while those who choose the wicked way will perish. These are the natural outcomes of the ways that are chosen.

Our ministry then is to call those who have wandered from the Way to recommit their lives to following Jesus. May we wisely choose to be planted next to the river of living water, Jesus, and put down roots that will nurture and bless us for the rest of our lives.

CLOSING

"Let every student be plainly instructed, and earnestly pressed to consider well, (that) the main end of his life and studies is, to know God and Jesus Christ, which is eternal life, and therefore to lay Christ at the bottom as the only foundation of all sound knowledge and learning."[4]

Henry Dunster

JOHN MYLES

Church Planter

**The memorial to the First Baptist church in Wales
Ilston, Wales. (Judy and Bruce Pullen)**

JOHN MYLES (1621-83)

John Myles, a graduate of Brasenose College in Oxford, organized the first Baptist church in Wales at Ilston in 1645 and then four other churches in the area. In 1662, he fled taking with him the Ilston church records and some of the church members. They first settled in Rehoboth and then Swansea, Massachusetts.

John Myles was born in 1621 in Newton-Clifford, Herefordshire on the border between Wales and England. Myles was the ideal candidate for the Welsh mission since the English and Welsh languages and customs mingled there.

Brasenose College in Oxford where he began his studies in 1636 was a center for Puritans and perhaps it was here Myles became acquainted with the Baptist way. Upon graduation he may have become a chaplain with Cromwell's New Model Army in Wales or a tutor for one of the wealthy Welsh families.

With the death of King Charles and the rise to power of Oliver Cromwell and the Puritans, the kingdom made the radical conversion to a commonwealth. The conformists were out and the nonconformists were in. At the Ilston parish in Wales the Anglican clergyman, William Houghton, was removed as rector and eventually John Myles was installed.

In the spring of 1649 Myles, along with his friend, Thomas Proud, visited a Baptist Church in London that met in Glazier's Hall on Broad Street. The church had set aside a day for prayer and fasting for a proposed mission to plant a Baptist church in Wales. Myles and Proud responded to the call, were baptized by the church and commissioned to return to the Gower area in southern Wales to start Baptist churches there.

Sarah Williams and Margaret Davies were the first to be baptized. Others soon followed their lead. Later that year the Ilston congregation voted on October 1, 1649, to become a properly organized Baptist Church, the first in Wales.

The next year John Myles was offered a position as "Approver" under the Act for the Better Propagation and Preaching of the Gospel in Wales (1650). As a representative of the Parliament and Cromwell, he certified the Puritans who would replace the Anglicans in the Welsh parishes. Because Baptists believe in the separation of church and state, Myles was criticized for receiving compensation from the state. Clergy in the free church tradition were to be supported by the congregation, not the state. Later, when the monarchy was restored, Myles was threatened with imprisonment for being a representative of the Cromwell government.

The Christian faith had taken root in Wales a thousand years before, planted there by Illtud who, converted by Cadoc, a Christian hermit, established a Celtic monastery where he trained leaders such as Samson and Gildas, the first Welsh historian. The Celtic pastor,

Iltud, cultivated the soil in which the Baptist pastor, John Myles, planted his churches.

The Ilston congregation met in the parish church until May 29, 1660, when, with the return of the monarchy and the state church, they were evicted. At that time it is believed they moved to a vacant, secluded thirteenth century chapel known as "Trinity Well." The chapel which probably belonged to Major-General Rowland Dawkins, an old friend of John Myles, was used for three years until persecution drove the congregation underground. The ruins of this old chapel have been maintained as a memorial to those first heroic Welsh Baptists.

Ilston was the first of several tightly knit churches formed under Myles leadership. Other church plants were at Hay-on-Wye (1650), Llantrisant (1650), Carmarthen (1651) and Abergavenny (1652). Worship services were held in both Welsh and English on Sundays. During the week disciples were nurtured in homes in the different villages. With Ilston as the mother church, Myles organized a rotating preaching schedule for the other churches who, although they met separately, gathered at Ilston on the third Sunday of the month to break bread together. Communion, as Myles understood it, was for believers who had been baptized by immersion and had covenanted together to form a community of faith. By 1653 the other congregations were established enough to launch out on their own and by the end of the next year a church start in Swansea was proposed with rotating preachers. Membership at Ilston rose to 261.

The churches cooperated in three areas: providing advice in controversial matters, in financially supporting mission churches, and in joint planning. The General Meeting or Association had no right to intervene in the life of a member congregation without that congregation's express invitation, a policy continued by Baptists today.

With the death of Oliver Cromwell in 1658, the golden days for Baptists were coming to a close. When the Commonwealth folded, Myles was forced to resign and William Houghton returned as rector. When Myles left for New England, those who remained continued to meet under the leadership of Lewis Thomas until a new act in 1664 made it a crime to meet anywhere. Hunted and harassed, the congregation continued underground for the next 20-30 years eventually surfacing in Swansea as the Bethesda Baptist Church.

When John Myles, Thomas Proud, and a few friends fled the religious persecution in Wales with the Ilston church records, they headed for Boston. In 1663 they settled in the Plymouth Colony at Rehobath where they signed a covenant forming a Baptist church, the first in Massachusetts. Worship services were open to the villagers, even those Christians who held differing beliefs. Despite their ecumenical stance, the state church continued to persecute the tiny congregation. Although well accepted by the village, the authorities felt threatened and in 1667 fined and expelled Myles for gathering an unauthorized "publicke meeting."

The congregation moved to an area the natives called Wannamoiset, where they erected a meeting house. Later that year Plymouth colony permitted them to organize as a village which they called Swansea after the area they had left. The town was the first in the Commonwealth to grant religious freedom. The congregation adopted the name "the church of Christ in Swansea," and it admitted all who recognized Jesus as Lord and Savior, "although differing from us in such controversial points as are not absolutely and essentially necessary to salvation."

An educator, Myles early in 1674 organized a village school open to all free of charge. For many years he was its only teacher. After the death of his first wife, John Myles married Anne Humphreys, whose father was a magistrate in the Massachusetts colony.

Within the congregation were both General and Particular Baptists. Eventually the General Baptists separated in 1680, gathering a group that laid hands on the newly baptized and refused to sing during worship. After a few years of informal worship, they organized and called a pastor.

During King Philip's War, the Swansea church was closed. The Wampanoag tribe in 1675 under the leadership of King Philip, went on a three-year rampage destroying twenty towns in New England, killing 15 percent of the white male population. During those war years Myles moved to Boston where he briefly served Boston's First Baptist Church. His house in Swansea became the town garrison. After a new meeting house was erected at Tyler's Point, Myles returned to Swansea where he served the church until his death on February 3, 1683. Anne died ten years later.

By the time of his death there were four Baptist churches in the Commonwealth of Massachusetts: the two at Swansea, one in

Boston, and one on Martha's Vineyard at Gay Head organized by Peter Folger, the grandfather of Benjamin Franklin.

The records John Myles brought from Wales contained a covenant members had signed. Often churches organized around such a covenant and periodically would publically reaffirm it by reciting it in unison.

John Myles was an effective administrator, planting churches in Wales and then in Massachusetts. Today the office of the Baptist Union of Wales in Swansea is named Ty Ilston (Ilston House) honoring the first mission to plant a Baptist church in Wales.

TRAVEL NOTES: BRASENOSE COLLEGE, OXFORD

From Radcliffe Square in the heart of Oxford we entered Brasenose College through a tall, sixteenth century gatehouse. Passing through the massive, wooden doors, we found ourselves in the old quad, an area familiar to John Myles. For protection most of the colleges were formed in a quadrangle with one entrance and a courtyard in the center; Brasenose is no exception. A couple of ducks were wandering around the green; an ancient sun dial painted on one of the buildings marks the afternoon hour, as it might have when John Myles was a student here. Glancing back, we spied the towering dome of the Bodleian Library which we had just visited.

The Brasenose name, first recorded in 1270, was probably derived from a "brass nose" or knocker which hung on the door of the medieval Oxford hall and offered sanctuary to those who rang it. An ancient knocker, a genuine twelfth century "brazen nose" hangs in the hall, a living link with the oldest period of university history.

Little is known about the original hall. Legend has it that the ninth century Celtic theologian, John Scotus Erigena, studied there. In 1509 under the leadership of a lawyer and a bishop Brasenose Hall, which had been just a living area for students, was transformed into Brasenose College.

The librarian guided us around the grounds. In the library she showed us some old racquets that students used to play badminton on rainy days in the library.

TRAVEL NOTES: SWANSEA, WALES.

It's Sunday and we are in Swansea, Wales. After a few misses and wrong turns we found the Pantygwydr Baptist Church. Geoff

Fewkes and Pete Orphan, who is a chaplain at the university, were the pastors of this active and inviting Welsh congregation. Communion, traditionally served on the third Sunday of the month, was part of the service as was a dedication of parents and children. After worship we joined the congregation for a coffee hour where we met Pat Moore who volunteered to show us the way to Nicholaston House, a former hotel and now Christian retreat center, where we were to stay.

After lunch with Pat at the Gower Inn in Ilston, we walked down the shady path in the woods nearby to the site of the first Baptist Church. A small bridge arches over a meandering stream. Some of the foundation of the chapel remains. An iron fence once surrounded the site, but all that is left now are its four brick corner posts. A memorial pulpit surmounted by an open Bible holds a tablet that reads, in part,

> "To commemorate the foundation in this valley of the First Baptist Church in Wales 1649-1660, and to honor the memory of its founder, John Myles. This ruin is the site of the pre-reformation chapel of Trinity Well and is claimed by tradition as a meeting place of the above Cromwellian Church."

Former Prime Minister David Lloyd George, a Welsh Baptist, visited here in 1928 to unveil the memorial. We spent five days at Nicholaston House enjoying the rocky coast and the sea air in "one of the five most scenic places in Britain."

Three years later we returned to spend time in this delightful place. It was at Nicholaston House that we met Gary and Jane Gregor. Gary was a source of information about John Myles' years in Wales. Together we visited Baptist sites in the Swansea area including the Bethesda Baptist Church, a historic church which has been abandoned and is slowly deteriorating.

TRAVEL NOTES: SWANSEA, MASSACHUSETTS.

The congregation John Myles planted is still in existence. In the spring I visited the church. Howard Levine, the church moderator, was my guide as we visited a variety of sites. The meeting house was built in 1848. The small, white colonial structure sits on a slight knoll overlooking an old graveyard filled with headstones worn by the weather. The worship area is almost square. The colonial style pews still have doors. On the back wall is a memorial plaque that reads,

"A tablet placed by a committee of American members of the Gower Society of Swansea, Wales, Edgar Davies, chairman, San Diego, California. 1663-1963. Commemorating the establishment of the First Baptist Church of Swansea, Massachusetts by John Myles - Pastor and others of the First Baptist Church of Wales. This is the First Church of any denomination founded on the American Continent by Welshmen. The founders' church was at Ilston on the Gower Peninsula."

We first visited the site where a stone marker reads,

"Near this spot stood the John Myles Garrison House, the place of meeting of the troops of Massachusetts Bay and Plymouth colonies, commanded by Major Thomas Savage and James Cudworth, who marched to the relief of Swansea, at the opening of King Philips' War, A.D. 1675."

Then we found the stone marking the site where the original chapel stood. The tablet reads,

"The First Baptist Church in Massachusetts was founded near this spot A.D.1663. Rev. John Myles, James Brown, Joseph Carpenter, Benjamin Alby, Nicholas Tanner, Eldad Kingsley, John Butterworth, Founders."

TRAVEL NOTES: JOHN HAY LIBRARY

The John Hay Library stores Brown University's special collections. The Swansea church trusts the library with its original membership directory. After being given permission to photograph the directory and to obtain pages from its microfilm copy, I contacted Mark Brown, curator of manuscripts, who made the resources readily available.

I was thrilled to hold and then photograph this ancient document and to know it includes the names of the pioneer Baptists who first formed a Baptist church in Massachusetts. The book is bound in soft yellow parchment. One of the covers is in the form of an extended flap bearing a metal clasp intended for a fastener on the other. The ink has bled through the paper making the handwriting difficult to read. (Photograph on page 46)

REFLECTIONS ON COVENANT - Hebrews 10:16-25

"This is the covenant that I will make with them after those days, says the Lord: I will put my laws in their hearts, and I will write them on their minds. . . . I will remember their sins and their lawless deeds no more." Hebrews 10:16.

This quotation from Jeremiah by the author of Hebrews is given in two parts: the first proclaims the new covenant and the second a new level of forgiveness through the sacrifice of Jesus. Then with his central theological argument concluded, the author launches into its practical aspects. The annual privilege of the high priest, encountering God in the temple, is now the daily privilege of every member of the community of faith. We may go directly to Jesus in prayer. Then he encourages us to hold on to the hope we professed when we were baptized. Finally, we are called to love and encourage one another.

What is a covenant? A covenant is a solemn promise or agreement by a community of faith to walk in the Way of Jesus. The early Christians saw themselves as a community bound together by a covenant that was a free, creative reinterpretation of the older traditions. They spoke of a new covenant sealed with the blood of Jesus. The Sinai covenant established a community based on the Ten Commandments; the new covenant created a community based on the commandment to love God and love people.

CLOSING

The churches in Rehobath, Swansea and Boston organized around a covenant. Baptist congregations create church covenants to succinctly express what it means to be a loving and purposeful people of God. A clearly phrased, meaningful covenant used in a significant way by a dedicated congregation may just be the springboard for meaningful ministry and mission.

Many Baptist congregations, having organized around a covenant, still traditionally reaffirm that covenant with God and each other during the service in which they also celebrate communion. Whereas covenants in the past were often lengthy and detailed, the revised covenants of many contemporary churches are succinct and to the point, written in a style that is clearly understood and easily read. Covenants express how Christians agree to live together in Jesus.

Here is a contemporary covenant for your contemplation.

COVENANT [1]

"Having been led by the Spirit of God to love and follow Jesus Christ, we do now joyfully covenant with God and each other:

to walk together in Christian love;
to worship God, observing the Lord's Supper and Baptism;
to commit ourselves to prayer and Bible study;
to love and forgive others, as God loves and forgives us;
to pray for and help others in times of sickness and distress;
to contribute cheerfully to the mission of the church;
to share our faith with our families, friends, and neighbors;
to pray and work for a spirit of unity among all Christians;
to strive for justice, freedom, and peace in our world; and
to join with some other Christian Church when we move from this community.

In every area of our lives, we will strive to do God's will to the honor and glory of Jesus Christ, our Lord and Savior. Amen!"

- 9 -

JOHN BUNYAN

The Progress of a Pilgrim

The Statue of John Bunyan in Bedford, England

62

JOHN BUNYAN (1628-88)

John Bunyan, the popular author of the *Pilgrim's Progress, Grace Abounding*, and other books, was encouraged by a Baptist congregation in Bedford to be baptized and to preach. When the Commonwealth ended and royalty was restored, Bunyan was thrown in jail for preaching the gospel. There he wrote *Pilgrim's Progress*, which, published in 1678, became a favorite companion to the Bible.

John Bunyan was born to Thomas and Mary Bunyan in 1628 and christened in the conformist chapel at Elstow. The Bunyans lived near there in the last cottage down a country lane called Bunyan's End on land owned by the family for generations. Adjoining the old, thatched roofed cottage, was a workshop housing a forge which Bunyan's father, Thomas, a tinker by trade, used to mend pots and pans. Their income was supplemented with food from farming and fish from the River Ouse.

John was privileged to attended a local school where he learned to read and write. Through the popular books his grandfather sold from town to town, a whole new world of stories of saints slaying dragons and other such monsters was opened to him. In his teens he joined his father as a tinker, making and selling wares in the Bedford area. The variety of people he met and the sites he saw were all fuel for the writer's fire.

It was an age of turmoil as the conformist churches sought to control the free churches. By law, everyone was to belong to the state church and take communion in it three times a year. All other forms of worship were banned including Roman Catholic. During this period thousands of Baptists and Roman Catholics would be accused of treason and punished for freely exercising their faith. When they could take it no longer, Civil War erupted, the state church was overthrown, and the Puritan spirit dominated Britain for the next fifteen years allowing the free churches to flourish.

Bunyan joined the army where he came into contact with committed Christians. Discharged after three years, he returned home to pick up his trade and marry. His wife, a Christian, brought her Bible and a couple of religious books. Their first child, Mary, was born blind. They were to have three more before Bunyan's wife died a decade later. He then married Elizabeth who supported him during his years in jail.

Bunyan tells us in *Grace Abounding* that he struggled with the state of his soul. He heard voices calling to him, "Wilt thou leave thy sins and go to Heaven, or have thy sins and to Hell?" He wanted to go to heaven, but did not know the way. This experience, finding the way to God, was the theme of *Pilgrim's Progress.*

According to his understanding of Calvin, most people were doomed from birth to end in Hell, no matter what they did on earth. Relatively few were predestined to be the "chosen," to be the Elect who would go to Heaven to enjoy eternal life. And so he asked how did one know if one were chosen? He gave up bell-ringing, swearing, playing games, and dancing, yet he found no joy in his religious quest.

One day in Bedford he met a small group of women who seemed to have that joy. They belonged to a small Baptist congregation, Bedford Meeting, gathered by John Gifford. His discussions of the Bible with them led him to studying an old tattered copy of Martin Luther's *Commentary on Galatians.* His spirit soared when he found in it a description of his own condition and the way to overcome it. At the age of 25, Bunyan gave his life to Jesus and was baptized by Pastor Gifford in the River Ouse. Called to preach by the congregation, his vivid style of painting word pictures made the gospel understandable. People were drawn to him by the spell of his stories.

The Bunyans moved from Elstow to a little cottage in Bedford where he continued in the tinker trade but also often preached to religious gatherings. When Pastor John Gifford died later that year, Bunyan became even more active. He published a few tracts (*A Few Sighs from Hell* and *Some Truths Open*) which were probably based on his sermons.

For seven years all went well until Charles II returned and assumed the throne. The Royalists once again controlled the country and ruled the state church. Everything possible was done to eliminate or at least drastically reduce the influence of the Puritan spirit that had soared over Britain for the past twenty years. The Royalists wanted their revenge. A new Act of Uniformity was passed which prohibited any religious meetings by the free churches and required membership and attendance in the conformist churches. The Bedford Meeting was expelled from the building in which it worshiped. Within the year Bunyan was arrested for preaching in a farmhouse not far from Bedford. So at the age of 32, given the choice to stop preaching or to go to jail, John Bunyan chose the Bedford county jail where he remained for twelve years, despite Elizabeth's constant pleas for his release.

The jails of his day were foul and filthy beyond belief with no sanitation. The food was meager and the sexes were not separated. Prisoners slept on straw. Visitors dipped their handkerchiefs in turpentine to avoid the smell when visiting. In winter it was freezing, in summer steaming hot. A long jail sentence was often a death sentence as it had been for Thomas Helwys. Bunyan survived with the help of God and his loving wife.

Bunyan's life had changed direction after he was baptized and now it had changed once more with his imprisonment. For him it became a time of meditation and study. He was allowed a Bible. Many of the prisoners were there for their religious beliefs so Bunyan gathered them for worship on a regular basis. He would take a text from the Bible and "fly off" with it. Some sermons he recorded and eventually published. He described himself as the "Lord's free prisoner," having time to do the things he most wanted to do without interruption. He was allowed to have food brought, and his little blind daughter, Mary, brought him soup. He completed several books (*Prison Meditations; The Holy City*; and *Grace Abounding to the Chief of Sinners*) during these years and saw them published. He started *Pilgrim's Progress* during this period but was released in 1672 before it was completed. Charles II, wanting to encourage Roman Catholics, proclaimed religious toleration for all and allowed those who were jailed for religious beliefs to be released. Chapels reopened and pastors returned to their congregations. In thankfulness Bunyan wrote a tract in praise of the King, an act he was soon to regret.

Returning home to Elizabeth and the children, Bunyan was called to the pastorate where he would spend the rest of his life. His reputation grew through his writing and preaching, and he was even invited to preach in London. Within three years, fearing a renewed Roman Catholic presence, the Act of Indulgence was rescinded and the Act of Uniformity once again strictly enforced. Bunyan broke the law repeatedly by preaching to his congregation and was once again tried, convicted, and jailed. His stay was only six months but it was long enough to finish his masterpiece, *Pilgrim's Progress*, a vision of life told allegorically as if it were a journey. Published in 1678, the first two editions sold out by the end of the year. He added a sequel, *Pilgrim's Progress, Part II*, which told of the travels of the Pilgrim's wife, Christina, and their children as they followed in

Christian's footsteps on his pilgrimage. In the sequel are found some of Bunyan's finest verses. These words have been sung by congregations around the world:

> Who would true valour see Let him come hither;
> One here will constant be, Come wind come weather
> There's no discouragement, Shall make him once relent,
> His first avowed intent To be a pilgrim.[1]

Released once again from prison, this time through the efforts of the great Oxford theologian, Dr. John Own, Bunyan continued to write, publish, and preach. He helped license more than 25 pastors and 30 places of worship in the area. As a result he became known as "Bishop" Bunyan even though Baptists do not have bishops.

Bunyan was open and loving toward all true and sincere Christians. Many of the Baptist churches of the day practiced closed communion as some still do, that is, they would not allow anyone to take communion who had not experienced baptism as a believer. While Bunyan recognized communion as one of God's ordinances, he did not "make an idol of it." He allowed other Christians to participate in the Lord's Supper and defended his position in his book, *Differences in Judgement About Water Baptism No Bar to Communion*, in which he wrote "The Church of Christ hath not warrant to keep out of their communion the Christian that is discovered to be a visible saint by the word, the Christian that walketh according to his light with God."

His end came suddenly. He went to help reconcile a father and son, then rode 40 miles to London in the rain. Catching a cold, he nevertheless responded to the invitation to preach at a Baptist meetinghouse in Whitechapel on Sunday. His sermon encouraged Christians to love one another. He said: "If you are the children of God, live together lovingly. If the world quarrel with you it is no matter; but it is sad if you quarrel together." [2] This was his last sermon. He died of pneumonia on August 31, 1688, and was buried in Bunhill Fields, the free church burial grounds.

Bunyan lived to see some sixty of his writings in print. At the time of his death more than 100,000 copies of *Pilgrim's Progress* had been sold, some as far as New England. Today it has been translated in to more than 165 languages and, at one time, was second in sales only to the Bible.

TRAVEL NOTES: BEDFORD.

It was raining lightly when we drove to Bedford in south-central England where John Bunyan lived. The city now recognizes him as one of their most famous residents. We walked to the town center to see an imposing statue honoring Bunyan. On its square base are scenes from *Pilgrim's Progress.*

A small Bunyan Museum is located in the Bunyan Meeting House. It includes copies of his books and some of his personal property. The day ended as we drove to Elstow where we took pictures of Moot Hall where it is said Bunyan had lived.

TRAVEL NOTES: BUNHILL FIELDS, LONDON.

On our first day in London we drove to the old burial ground of Bunhill Fields. Long before 1549 when the first wagon load of bones was delivered for burial from the overflowing charnel house in St. Paul's Churchyard, the field had been given the name Bone Hill. From 1665 to 1852 when it was finally closed, 120,000 were buried there.

In this peaceful spot, shaded by trees, and surrounded by pleasant walks are located the tombs of John Bunyan; Hanserd and Anne Knollys; poet and artist William Blake; Susanna Wesley, the mother of John and Charles Wesley; Daniel Defoe; and other free church Christians of their day. Today this is a delightful park where people walk and enjoy a lunch break before returning to work.

REFLECTIONS ON CHRISTIAN WRITING - Luke 1:1-4.

John Bunyan spoke the truth as he understood it. Rather than betray what he believed, he spent time in jail. Luke wrote in his gospel about the truth so that "those who love God" might better understand the truth about Jesus. Luke also knew what it meant to sacrifice for what he believed. Inspired to write a life of Jesus for those who love God and read Greek, Luke shared the faith he had come to hold with the world in which he moved.

Luke began by stating that what he had been inspired to write is the result of careful historical research. Competent writers research a project, gathering information about their subject. In the process doors open, paths are provided, and ways are given to express their thoughts. Inspiration comes as the writer is open to God's leading.

Luke was engaged in accurately writing down in a certain order what he had heard from eyewitnesses in order to accomplish the goal of enabling those who love God to come to a faith in Jesus as Lord and Savior. Christian writers attempt to clearly and convincingly relate their faith so that inquiring readers who are seeking a way of life may share the journey of faith with them.

In the first year of its existence The Baptist Tract Society, realizing the impact of Bunyan on the world, published a *Life of Bunyan*. The Christian writing ministry continues to flourish today as writers seek to share their faith.

CLOSING

In *Pilgrim's Progress* as Christian "came to the foot of the Hill *Difficulty*; at the bottom of which was a spring. . . . *Christian* now went to the spring, and drank thereof, to refresh himself, and then began to go up the hill, saying –

> The hill, though high, I covet to ascend,
> The difficulty will not me offend;
> For I perceive the way to life lies here.
> Come, pluck up heart, let's neither faint for fear'
> Better, though difficult, the right way to go,
> Than wrong, though easy, where the end is woe."

John Bunyan [3]

10

BENJAMIN KEACH

The Joy of Music

Benjamin Keach

BENJAMIN KEACH (1640-1704)

Benjamin Keach was the pastor of the Horsleydown Church in Southwark, near Shakespeare's Globe theater, for more than thirty years. He was a powerful preacher, prolific writer including hymns, and is credited with introducing hymn singing to English congregations.

Benjamin Keach was born in Stoke Hammond, England on February 29, 1640 to John and Fedora Keach. Raised an Anglican, he became a Baptist in his teens. He soon began preaching in the General Baptist congregation near his home in Winslow and eventually was called to be its pastor (1663-1668). When he turned twenty, he married Jane Grove with whom he had five children before she died ten years later.

When Charles II resumed the throne in 1660, the state churches once again regained their power to force people to conform to their traditions. In 1664 Keach wrote *The Child's Instructor: Or, a New and Easy Primer*, a basic school book of religious instruction for children. Because he advocated in it that only believers should be baptized, he was arrested and found guilty of being "a heretical . . . person." His punishment was to stand in a pillory for two hours in Aylesbury and Winslow on successive Saturdays where his banned books would be burned in front of him. When the curious crowd gathered, he preached, sharing his convictions until they threatened to gag him. Years later he rewrote the book from memory, sold it at the church's bookstore, and was arrested once again. This time his punishment was a fine of £20, a considerable sum for a poor Baptist preacher. Dr. John Roberts, a member of his congregation, paid it for him.

These were dangerous times. Twelve General Baptists sentenced to death that year were saved at the last moment by a wealthy Baptist merchant, William Kiffin, who personally interceded with the king. Although the burning of books instead of Baptists was a sign that religious freedom was coming, it certainly had not yet arrived.

No longer comfortable in Winslow, the Keachs sold their belongings and journeyed by coach to London (1668), only to be stopped by highwaymen and robbed. In London they joined a small General Baptist house church in Southwark where Keach was ordained an elder. After Jane died, Keach married Susannah Partridge in a ceremony officiated by Hanserd Knollys. Now influential in the organization of the Particular Baptists, Knollys probably convinced Keach to become one also. Several Baptist congregations adopted Calvinistic beliefs and affirmed them in the First London Confession (1644).

Splitting from the General Baptist congregation, Keach gathered a congregation in Horsleydown. He served the church for over thirty years, becoming a leading Baptist theologian, prolific hymn writer, and a powerful preacher. The Metropolitan Tabernacle traces its roots through Spurgeon (see chapter twelve) to this congregation and lists Keach as one of its early pastors. Despite his Calvinistic stance, his preaching was characterized by a warm, inviting appeal to trust in Jesus. Charles Spurgeon called his predecessor's style, "intensely direct, solemn, and impressive." The small meeting house they first erected soon grew to hold more than a thousand persons.

Benjamin Keach pioneered a Baptist catechism that was widely used. He argued with the Quakers and constantly challenged both the Anglicans and the Puritans. He advocated the laying on of hands at the time of baptism as General Baptists did, but he wrote about Calvinistic Baptist church polity. He defended the Calvinistic perspective on salvation when it was attacked. He opposed Baptist churches worshiping on the "Seventh Day." As did Bunyan, he published popular religious allegories such as *The Travels of True Godliness*. He advocated adequate financial support for pastors in his book, *The Gospel Minister's Maintenance Vindicated* (1689). He is credited with writing more than fifty books including several collections of sermons.

His son, Elias Keach (1667-1701), sailed for Philadelphia when he was twenty. He gathered a congregation at Pennepek in 1688 and, with that as a base, traveled to towns in the Trenton and Philadelphia areas preaching to groups of British settlers. The churches he helped found adopted his father's Articles of Faith (1697) and remained in contact with each other when Elias left for home in 1692. They eventually formed the Philadelphia Baptist Association in 1707.

Benjamin Keach will forever be associated with the controversy over hymn singing that split the London congregations. Although hymns and psalms were sung occasionally by English congregations, Benjamin Keach was the first to introduce their regular use in English congregational worship. Beginning in 1673 the congregation sang a hymn at the conclusion of communion as the disciples had done after the last supper. Some members disliked the innovation and left, including Isaac Marlow, a successful jeweler, who went on to write several books opposing the singing of hymns in worship.

The battle raged over the next ten years with books authored on both sides, tearing the London Baptist community into two camps. The Baptists were divided and disorganized. Good friends, Hanserd Knollys and William Kiffin took opposing stances on this issue.

Although most of the opposition's arguments would seem ridiculous to us today, they were taken seriously then.

The 1689 Particular Baptist assembly voted to allow individual congregations to sing hymns without censure from the other congregations. Two years later Keach brilliantly defended his positions with *The Breach Repaired in Gods Worship* (1691), arguing both scripturally, "we are called to sing God's praises," and practically, "hymns are useful for Christian education," that hymn singing is a form of spiritual renewal. "It is not too much to claim that on March 1, 1691, when Keach's church voted to sing a hymn each Sunday following the sermon, the great tradition of English Protestant hymnody began." [1]

Keach published two hymnals, *Spiritual Melody* (1691) and *Spiritual Songs* (c.1696). The churches that sang hymns flourished; those that did not declined. Today we still have worship wars over our music.

In his faith journey Benjamin Keach remained firm in his convictions while remaining conscious of what was essential and what was not. He disagreed with other Baptists including the General Baptists and the Seventh Day Baptists, but he continued to build bridges with them, reminding everyone of the importance of loving other Christians with "that catholic (universal) love that should run in all the veins of everyone that is born of God." He led a campaign for better maintenance of the ministry and better training. He encouraged the "congregations of baptized believers in England and Wales" to invite their young people to become pastors using scripture, reason and wit convincingly. He died on July 18, 1704 and is buried in the cemetery of his first congregation in Winslow.

Baptists today are seeking ways to move forward in the midst of conflict and uncertainty. Benjamin Keach modeled a conciliatory spirit toward those who differed with him. Congregations today often try to minimize conflict over hymns by mixing the music they sing using hymns and songs from the styles of classic, gospel, praise and contemporary music.

TRAVEL NOTES: SOUTHWARK.

A meeting house built in Goat's Yard Passage, Horse-lie-down (now Horsleydown) and expanded over the years, eventually held more than a thousand persons. It was first replaced on the site by a large brewery and then by offices and apartments. The congregation eventually ended up at Maze Pond which is now the site of Guy's Hospital parking lot.

TRAVEL NOTES: PRINCETON, NEW JERSEY

A special collection of Benjamin Keach's sermons and hymns are found in the Speer Library on the Princeton Seminary campus. Several days were spent researching this book there.

REFLECTIONS ON CHURCH MUSIC - Psalm 98: 4-6

The Psalms is the songbook of the Old Testament people. Psalm 98 calls for joyous singing in the celebration of God. In the seventeenth century English congregations sang only psalms.

Benjamin Keach introduced the singing of hymns that witness to the faith (some of which he wrote), at the close of the celebration of the Lord's Supper. It would seem likely that he based this on Matthew 26: 26-30. After celebrating the Passover in Jerusalem, Jesus and his disciples closed this emotional time together with a hymn before once again facing the forces that would seek to destroy the Way. The earliest Christian churches held the conviction that the meal Jesus celebrated with his disciples was a foretaste of heaven when all of God's people will join Jesus around the table.

CLOSING

Although Benjamin Keach is remembered for his advocacy of hymn singing, it is rare to find one he wrote in a hymnal now. You might try your hand at writing a hymn as I have. Begin by choosing a hymn tune that you like that is not too familiar (don't choose *Amazing Grace*), and try writing words to it. Having a theme helps. Below is a hymn that I wrote to the tune, "Ash Grove," for the Renewed for Mission emphasis of the American Baptist Churches. It has been sung at several Biennials and regional meetings and in numerous congregations. Permission is granted to reprint the words for use by your congregation. Please tell me if you use it.

Dr. Bruce Reed Pullen
(brpabc@aol.com)

The Call to Renewal

1. The call to renewal is heard thru our churches
   as we seek new life thru the Spirit of God.
Our journey together has led us to growing
   in caring and sharing our new life in God.

Refrain. Our God will renew us, restore, and refresh us,
   revive and rekindle the flame in our heart.
Renewed in our mission, redeemed by our Savior,
   we pray for the courage to make a fresh start.

2. The call to renewal is a call to recite
   the story of Jesus, his word and his way.
Our journey together has led us to recalling
   the memories we share and the words that we say.

3. The call to renewal is a call to revival
   of worship and witness, of service and grace.
Our journey together has led us to embracing
   each one of God's children regardless of race.

11

ANDREW FULLER

A Passion for Mission

Andrew Fuller's desk

ANDREW FULLER (1754-1815)

Andrew Fuller, together with William Carey and others, founded the Baptist Missionary Society. He remained its secretary until his death in 1815.

Although Andrew Fuller was born February 7, 1754, in Wickham in Cambridgeshire, East Anglia, his family soon moved to a farm in Soham near Ely. His parents were both Baptists. Growing up, sports, especially wrestling, were an important part of his active life. He struggled to educate himself, reading everything available, including the popular works of John Bunyan. Challenged by Bunyan's writings to become a Christian, he struggled with what it means to live the Christian life.

"One winter evening I remember going with a number of other boys to a smith's shop, to warm ourselves by his fire. Presently they began to sing vain songs."[1] Feeling uncomfortable, he left, walking home wondering how he could find peace with God.

Encouraged by Pastor Eve to commit his life to Christ and prepare for the ministry, Andrew Fuller was baptized in the river in 1770. In 1774 he was ordained and a year later he succeeded his mentor as pastor in Soham. During that first year he married Sarah Gardiner. As it is for most pastors, the first years were a struggle as he learned from experience, but Fuller became a devoted and faithful pastor and preacher. Influenced by the ministry of Jonathan Edwards, he began his gradual movement toward evangelical preaching.

Although reluctant to leave Soham, Andrew Fuller accepted a call to Kettering in October 1782, but not before he sought the advice of other pastors in the association. Kettering at that time was a small market town with a population of around 3,000. His pastoral preaching, focusing on applying a Biblical text to life, revived life in the congregation. A prolific writer, he is credited with crushing hyper-Calvinism with a more moderate evangelical approach. "I do not believe everything that Calvin taught, nor any thing because he taught it." [2] The common understanding of Calvinist theology was that only the elect could be saved and that was predetermined so there was no need to invite anyone to follow Jesus. As one of the outstanding Baptist theologians of his day, he argued for a wider view of the redemptive work of God and the necessity for the churches to be involved in missions, offering salvation to all. His advocacy of the modern mission movement found a willing partner in William Carey.

Andrew Fuller had a passion for mission not only for the people in the parish but those around the world. His famous book, *The Gospel Worthy of all Acceptation, or the duty of sinners to believe in Jesus Christ,* (1785) called people to preach the gospel in the far corners of the world. In it he wrote, "the way to Jesus is open and free for whosoever will without exception." In this he was influenced by the revivalist pastor, Jonathan Edwards, from Northampton, Massachusetts who wrote *Inquiry into the Freedom of the Will.* "There can be no doubt that Edwards was the chief architect of the theological structures erected by Evangelicals in the Reformed tradition."[3]

The year 1792 marked significant changes in Fuller's life. Both Sarah, his wife, and Beeby Wallis, the senior deacon who was mainly responsible for his coming to Kettering, died. It was also the year that twelve other clergy and laymen gathered to organize the Baptist Missionary Society, the first voluntary Christian missionary society.

In 1794 Andrew Fuller, now 40 years old, married a pastor's daughter, Ann Coles. He remained at Kettering for more than thirty years during which time he traveled extensively in Great Britain and Ireland seeking support for the mission of the society. He was one of the most popular speakers of his day in Baptist and other independent churches. The General and Particular Baptist Churches drew closer together during those years as a result of their common commitment to overseas missions. Fuller's work influenced Charles Spurgeon to become more evangelical. His evangelical form of Calvinism became nicknamed "Fullerism." Princeton University (1798), Yale University (1805) and Brown University in Rhode Island all awarded him Doctor of Divinity degrees. He died of tuberculosis on Sunday, May 7, 1815 and more than 2,000 attended the funeral.

THE BAPTIST MISSIONARY SOCIETY

In May 1792 William Carey preached at the Association meeting in Nottingham on a text from Isaiah calling God's people to "Enlarge the place of your tent." The Great Commission was meant not only for disciples then, but for disciples now. We should, he preached, "Expect great things; attempt great things." Although the sermon touched their hearts, it had no immediate response. Frustrated with the apathy, Carey contacted Fuller to ask him for support in doing something. Fuller agreed to invite pastors to meet in Kettering to form "A Baptist Society for Propagating the Gospel among the Heathen." The pastors met at the home of Deacon Beeby Wallis's widow and agreed to pray for and support financially the dream of sending a missionary. Fuller passed his snuff box as an offering plate receiving more than £13 in pledges. William Carey promised the proceeds from his book, *The Enquiry*. Samuel Pearce's congregation in Birmingham later gave £70. William Staughton, a student, committed his preaching fees.

Fuller later wrote of the event that we were "somewhat like a few men, who were deliberating about the importance of penetrating into a deep mine, which had never before been explored. We had no one to guide us; and, while we were thus deliberating, Carey, as it were, said, 'Well I will go down if you will hold the rope.' But before he went down, he, as it seemed to me, took an oath from each of us at the mouth of the pit to this effect that while we lived, we should never let go the rope. You understand me. There was great responsibility attached to us who began the business." [4] The new venture was underway and Fuller never let go of the rope.

In 1793 John Thomas, a Baptist surgeon who had recently returned from India, met with the society. Carey volunteered to return to India with him and they sailed in June 1793. Carey served for forty years. Pledged to "hold the ropes" Fuller remained the society's secretary until his death in 1815, raising funds and traveling extensively, including five trips to Scotland.

TRAVEL NOTES: KETTERING, ENGLAND.

Although Baptists have been worshiping in Kettering for more than 300 years, the current Victorian chapel, renamed Fuller Baptist Church in honor of Andrew Fuller, was built in 1861. Our guide, John Pemble, led us first to the Mission House, nicknamed the Gospel Inn, where the British Missionary Society was organized. The Baptist Housing Association converted the building into apartments for the elderly in 1979 but has maintained a small area commemorating the society's formation.

Fuller Baptist Church is located in the downtown area next to a small mall. The impressive and well-maintained sanctuary holds more than 1,000 persons. There is a large balcony and a stained glass window, dedicated to Andrew Fuller, that was installed in 1910. A coffee house ministry reaches out to the community.

The Heritage room in the church is filled with memorabilia including Fuller's pulpit, his desk accompanied by some of his sermon notes, and the communion table he used. In the small, inner courtyard lies the graves of Fuller and his second wife.

WILLIAM STAUGHTON - NEW JERSEY

William Staughton (1770-1829), the student present at that first mission meeting, eventually sailed for New Jersey where he became headmaster at an academy in Bordentown and then later a pastor in Burlington. Princeton awarded him a Doctor of Divinity degree.

In 1805 he was called to the First Baptist Church in Philadelphia, where he remained for 18 years. Staughton became a prime mover in support of the foreign mission organization which he served as president and secretary until his death. He wrote that the "fire of Missionary enterprise was lit within him in Widow Wallis's back parlour."

WILLIAM CAREY (1761-1834) - INDIA

The Baptist Missionary Society's first foreign missionary, William Carey, went to India where he combined his love of Jesus with a love of things botanical, eventually earning a significant income managing the Botanical Gardens there. He translated the Bible into Bengali and opened a college at Serampore. His witness influenced Adoniram Judson, a pioneer Baptist missionary.

William Carey began his life as a shoemaker. Another apprentice, John Warr, shared his faith with him and eventually Carey was converted. He was baptized by John Ryland on October 5, 1783, in the river Nen.

A small Baptist church in Moulton called Carey to the pastorate where he refined his preaching skills. He caught a vision for foreign missions from Fuller, which he proclaimed to all, thus angering the Calvinist clergy. From Fuller's teachings he drew the inescapable conclusion that, if it is the duty of all to repent and believe the gospel, then it is also the responsibility of those entrusted with the gospel to carry it to the whole world.

In a sermon which includes the now famous lines, "Expect great things from God. Attempt great things for God," he urged Christians, especially Baptists, to come together around a united mission program. His proposal was simple, "Pray, Plan, and Pay." Not bad advice even for modern missions.

At the age of 32 Carey, his wife and three sons, left for India where he was to establish several Baptist churches. He was an evangelist, teacher, translator, publisher, and botanist.

ADONIRAM JUDSON (1788-1850) - BURMA

Carey, in turn, influenced Adoniram Judson. Judson was the son of a Congregational pastor, a graduate of Brown University and of Andover Seminary. The Congregationalists sent Judson and his wife, Ann, to India to plant churches there. Since the Baptists were already there in the person of William Carey, the Judsons realized they would need to defend their position on baptism. They spent much of their long sea voyage studying the Bible, and, soon after arriving in Calcutta, adopted Baptist principles and were immersed by Carey. They resigned their appointment and sought aid from Baptist churches in the United States.

Because of political difficulties, the Judsons were not allowed to stay in India, so on the advice of the Careys they left for Rangoon, Burma. Judson was a brilliant scholar and Bible translator. Ann was an ardent advocate of the Burma mission and often wrote to the states for support of their work. She worked tirelessly for the release of her husband when he was imprisoned during the Burmese war with England. Her biography was widely distributed as a role model for young women. They left behind a flourishing church that despite the political turmoil in Burma today continues.

REFLECTIONS ON MISSIONS - Isaiah 2:3 and Isaiah 54:2

Enlarge the site of your tent, and let the curtains of your dwelling be stretched out; do not hold back; lengthen your cords and strengthen your stakes (Isaiah 54:2).
Isaiah declares that all nations will eventually recognize God as supreme. People will be attracted to the places that worship God, will study God's word, and will act upon it, bringing justice and peace to the world.

At an association meeting William Carey had challenged the British Baptists by saying he was willing to go, if Andrew Fuller and the others would be willing to be his "rope holder (Isaiah 54:2)," and provide support for the mission. Carey spent the rest of his life in India as a missionary. His challenge then is a challenge to the church today to "lengthen its cords and strengthen its stakes" in a worldwide witness.

CLOSING

Andrew Fuller, preaching to the Nottingham Association in 1784, said: "If we compare the present state of things, or even the past, with the glorious prophecies of the Word of God, we cannot think, surely, that all is yet accomplished. By these prophecies, the Christian church is encouraged to look for great things at some period or other of her existence. . . . Let us take encouragement, in the present day of small things, by looking forward, and hoping for better days." [5]

Portrait of Andrew Fuller

Fuller Memorial Church in Kettering

CHARLES SPURGEON

The Prince of Preachers

Metropolitan Tabernacle, London

CHARLES HADDON SPURGEON (1834-92)

Charles Haddon Spurgeon was called in 1853 to the New Park Street Church in London. Within six years in order to hold the crowds his preaching attracted, the congregation built the Metropolitan Tabernacle. The Pastor's College he founded is now known as Spurgeon's College.

Charles Haddon Spurgeon was born in a small cottage in the rural village of Kelvedon in Essex on June 19, 1834, the eldest of the eight children of John and Eliza. The next year he went to live with his grandfather, James Spurgeon, who was the pastor of the Independent (Congregationalist) chapel in Stambourne for 58 years. There, from his grandparents, James and Anne, and from the Bible and books by Bunyan, Fox and others in the grandparent's library, Charles learned about the Christian faith. His grandmother gave him a penny for every Watts hymn he learned.

In 1841 at age seven he returned home. His father, John, was a bookkeeper in Colchester and preached Sundays in a small Separatist chapel ten miles away. On a wintry Sunday in January, 1850 instead of traveling with his father, Charles attended the nearest church, a Primitive Methodist chapel. It was to change his life. The snow delayed the pastor, so a deacon delivered a short, simple sermon to the 15 persons who had braved the storm. The text was Isaiah 45:22, "Look to me and be saved, all the ends of the earth, for I am God." Spurgeon did and he was. "I thought I could dance all the way home, and I could understand what John Bunyan meant when he declared he wanted to tell the crows on the fields about his conversion." [1] That evening he went along with his mother to a Baptist Chapel in Colchester.

He took delight in relating that while attending a Church of England school he became acquainted with the Anglican catechism. In response to the question, "What is required of a person to be baptized?" the answer was "repentance and faith." Convinced by the scriptures that he should be baptized as a believer, he sought out a retired Baptist missionary, the Reverend W. W. Cantlow. On his Mother's birthday, Friday, May 3, 1850, he was baptized at Isleham Ferry in the River Lark. "The wind blew down the river with a cutting blast as my turn came to wade into the flood, but after I had walked a few steps, and noted the people in the ferryboat, and in boats, and on either shore, I felt as if heaven and earth and all hell might gaze upon me, for I was not ashamed to own myself, there and then, a follower of the Lamb."[2]

Later that year after completing teacher training, he moved to Cambridge and taught in a private school and on Sundays at St. Andrews Street Baptist Church. Invited to go with another young man to lead services in a cottage in Teversham, he quickly discovered that each thought the other was to do the preaching. Nervously fingering his Bible, he preached his first sermon. Other sermons followed and soon he was called to pastor a church at Waterbeach. The attendance there soon tripled, filling the chapel. George Gould, impressed with his talk at a regional Sunday School Meeting in Cambridge, encouraged the deacons at New Park Street Church to invite Spurgeon to preach at the famous but declining church.

The New Park Street Church, soon to become the Metropolitan Tabernacle, traces its roots back to a General Baptist congregation first formed in 1652 during the Commonwealth era. The church split when its pastor, Benjamin Keach (1668 to 1704) became a Particular (Calvinist) Baptist. A new chapel on Carter Lane was built in 1757 while John Gill was pastor (1719-1771). John Rippon (1773-1836) succeeded him. Needing the land for an expansion of the London Bridge, the meeting house was demolished and the New Park Street Church, the largest Baptist chapel in Britain, was built in 1833. Both Gill and Rippon are buried in Bunhill Field.

Charles Haddon Spurgeon, age 19, accepted the invitation to preach at New Park Street Church. That evening in the congregation was Susannah Thompson, a charming young woman about his age. They met several times in the months ahead. He sent her a copy of *Pilgrim's Progress,* inscribed, "Miss Thompson, with desires for her progress in the blessed pilgrimage, from C. H. Spurgeon, April 20, 1854." She gave him a complete set of Calvin. On June 10 they attended the opening of the Crystal Palace and he proposed. On February 1, 1855, he baptized her in the New Park Street Chapel baptistry. They were married on January 8, 1856, at New Park Street and a Paris honeymoon followed. In September twin sons, Charles and Thomas, were born.

In 1857 they moved first to a rural ten room house in Nightingale Lane and then finally to Westwood where they remained the rest of their lives. Susannah developed the project of supplying books to ministers in need and during the next twenty years mailed more than 200,000 volumes.

Within weeks of his coming, the disheartened congregation sprang to life. Word spread of the great new preacher at New Park and the sanctuary which seated 1,200 was soon filled to overflowing. Following the traditional probationary period, the young minister was called to pastor the church. At first he allowed them to use the title "Reverend" but for the rest of his ministry he preferred to be known simply as pastor. Almost overnight by word of mouth Spurgeon became London's most popular preacher. He had an amazing gift of speech, employing simple, direct language, with a superb voice as clear as a bell. Services eventually had to be moved to Exeter Hall which seated 4,000 while New Park Street was being enlarged. Soon this building was also too small and they moved again, this time to Surrey Gardens Music Hall where he would preach to crowds of more than 10,000, quite a feat in a day when there were no sound systems. When the owners opened the amusement park in which the hall was located on Sundays, Spurgeon returned to Exeter Hall in protest. At the Crystal Palace in 1858 he preached to 23,000, a record-breaking crowd for the time.

The Metropolitan Tabernacle in Southwark was built and on March 31, 1861, the first services were held. He called it a tabernacle because they were to be a pilgrim congregation. The sanctuary had seats for 3,600, folding seats for another 1,000 and standing room for another 1,400, making it the largest free church in the world.

Although members were baptized by immersion as a witness to their faith in Jesus, the communion table was open to all believers. His brother, Dr. A. J. Spurgeon, became co-pastor in 1868, assuming the role of administrator and pastor while Charles concentrated on preaching and teaching. Pews were rented and there was no offering. Five minutes before the service those without passes were allowed to enter and fill the empty seats. After royalties from his writing came pouring in, he declined a salary.

Although devoted to the Puritan classics, Spurgeon was a product of revivalism. He touched the hearts of the people as no one else was doing. Influenced by Andrew Fuller, he preached that soul winning must be our passion. His passion for preaching grew out of his close walk with Jesus. His sermons were cabled to New York each Monday. In America he angered many in the South for his opposition to slavery. Smoking was thought by some to be a sin, but Spurgeon, who smoked a pipe, declared he smoked to the glory of God. He started a monthly magazine, The Sword and the Trowel, which continues to be part of the ministry of the Tabernacle today. The church reached out to widows and to children through an orphanage and the ministry continues today under the name Spurgeon's Childcare. Spurgeon compiled his sermons, wrote commentaries and developed devotional books. Today more titles by Spurgeon are in print than those of any other religious author, living or dead.

Although Baptists have been reluctant to adopt a creed, preferring to accept the Bible as their guide, over the years Baptists have been tempted to define who they are by forming some kind of creedal statement. In 1887 near the end of his life, ill and depressed, Spurgeon argued for the adoption by the Baptist Union of a creedal statement in order to define who were Christians and who were not. The Union had been founded in 1813 without a creed other than a statement about baptism of believers by immersion. The Council of the Baptist Union censured him, marking an unfortunate event in an otherwise brilliant career. Spurgeon parted ways with the Union and also the London Baptist Association which he had helped found in 1865. The Metropolitan Tabernacle congregation withdrew from the Baptist Union, rejoined in 1955, and then withdrew once again in 1971. Spurgeon College which was founded by Spurgeon to train pastors rejoined in 1938 and is an active part of the Union today.

Spurgeon possessed a sense of humor that occasionally surfaced. When asked on an insurance form if he ever had fits, he wrote, only fits of laughter. Racked with kidney failure, Charles Haddon Spurgeon died at the age of 57 on January 31, 1892, while on vacation in the beautiful Riviera town of Mentone, in the south of France and was buried February 11, 1892 at West Norwood. His personal library, which contained one of the best private collections of Puritan literature in Britain, is now housed at William Jewel, a Baptist college in Missouri.

TRAVEL NOTES: METROPOLITAN TABERNACLE.

Sunday morning, we crossed the River Thames headed for Southwark (Suth-uck) seeking the church Spurgeon served. Rebuilt after being bombed during World War II, the pillared portico of the Metropolitan Tabernacle rises majestically in an area popularly known as the Elephant and Castle, after an old pub that had been located there. Its Grecian facade remains unchanged but behind it lies a modern sanctuary whose extensive glass windows allow streams of sunshine to flood the pews. Spurgeon believed the Greek design was appropriate since the New Testament was written in Greek.

The area is urban with heavy traffic even on Sunday. In the large entrance area which allows people to mingle, we were warmly greeted. The simple service combines preaching and prayers interspersed with hymns accompanied by an organ. There was no printed order of worship or choir. To our great disappointment the current pastor, Dr. Peter Masters, was absent and there was a substitute speaker from the states.

After worship Stewart Davis, the sound coordinator, gave us a quick tour of the building. A striking portrait and a bust of Spurgeon are in the hall, however the greatest memorial to the "Prince of Preachers" is found in the Tabernacle Bookshop where copies of his writings may be purchased. A quarterly catalog is printed with an extensive listing of historical sermons.

TRAVEL NOTES: SPURGEON'S COLLEGE.

South of London is Spurgeon's College. In search of a healthier spot Spurgeon moved to this hill south of London. His ministry had exploded. Thousands were coming to hear him preach. He needed trained pastors to assist him, so at the age of 22 he founded the Pastor's College, now known as Spurgeon's College. During his lifetime nearly 900 pastors were trained and 200 churches planted in Britain. Started in a home, it moved to the Tabernacle. Then in 1922 the college was given a Victorian house and estate at Falkland Park on South Norwood Hill near Westwood, Spurgeon's former home.

The grounds cover thirty acres and are beautifully landscaped. The stained glass window in the entrance area, blown out during World War II, was replaced by a striking new one with the motto of the college, "Et teneo et teneor" (I both hold and I am held), donated by the First Baptist Church in Tulsa, Oklahoma. The main library was built in 1937 and the College Chapel in 1957. Above the Chapel is the Heritage Room, which contains a vast amount of material related to Spurgeon's life including his writings, letters, newspaper articles, photographs, and portraits. Outside is a life-sized statue of Spurgeon that once stood in the Baptist House in London.

Judy Powles, the librarian, treated us to tea and gave us a copy of her book, *Forward in Faith - Spurgeon's College in South Norwood*. The college community today numbers more than 400 and is the largest British Baptist college.

REFLECTIONS ON PREACHING - Acts 16:25-34

The power of personality, preaching, and promise is found in Acts 16. The promise here is if you believe in Jesus, you will be saved. Paul lived it and preached it as did Charles Haddon Spurgeon. Spurgeon saw himself as a student of the heart who learned more from conversations with others than from reading. "His sermons retain their interest because they are filled with stories, examples, and anecdotes to illustrate his points." [3] They had a sense of authority, were creative, and were Christ-centered, all qualities of a great preacher. His sermons were usually 45-50 minutes in length and were based on texts taken from a Bible that was translated as accurately as possible. He commented that the best way to fill a place of worship was to preach the gospel "in a natural, simple, interesting, earnest way."[4]

Personal preparation was important. All through the week he would gather material for Sunday. Then on Saturday evening he would pull it all together. He would examine the text from various angles and jot down thoughts that came to mind. He would check the commentaries on the text and finally a sermon outline would emerge. Using a natural speaking style he preached extemporaneously without memorizing or using a manuscript. His sermons are filled with vivid illustrations and puns, which adapted for a new generation, would hold audiences today. Spurgeon told his students to "Seek the fire of Wesley, and the fuel of Whitefield." [5] His sermons always were based on scripture from which he would preach the Word. The great deep, rich resonant voice that could reach to the far corners of a hall is lost, but many of the sermons he preached have been saved and they are a resource for us today.

Spurgeon almost always closed his sermons with an invitation to come to Christ. "The ordinary sermon should always be evangelistic." [6] He once commented that preaching was like surgery; the idea was to save the patient. It mattered not if the preaching or surgery was brilliant if the sinner was lost or the patient died. Preaching for Spurgeon had a point; it was to encourage persons to become disciples of Jesus.

CLOSING

After seeing a lamplighter igniting the gas lamps along the hill near his home, he wished his ministry could be remembered as lighting the lamps of others so that they may shine for God! The fires he ignited continue to blaze today. He was the most famous preacher of his day and remains one of the most popular and influential Baptist preachers of all time.

**Charles Haddon Spurgeon
Statue at Spurgeon's College**

PART THREE

EPILOGUE

"The spider casts her film out to the wind,
feeling sure that some where or other
it will adhere and form
the beginning of her web.
She commits the slender filament to the breeze
believing that there is a place
provided for it to fix itself.
In this fashion we should believingly
cast forth our endeavors in this life,
confident that God will find a place for us.
He who bids us pray and work
will aid our efforts and guide us
in his providence in a right way.
Do not sit still in despair,
but keep casting out the floating thread
of hopeful endeavor,
and the wind of love
will bear it to its resting place." [7]

Charles Haddon Spurgeon

MAY THE DREAM NEVER DIE

that we can make a difference

The American Baptist Center in Valley Forge

Baptist churches in America are unique. Each congregation is different yet there are many similarities. Our roots reach back through the colonies to Britain where the first Christians began developing the convictions that have led to our being called Baptists. Although Baptists are characterized by baptism of believers by immersion, our distinctive identity lies in our doctrine of the church, its origin, nature, and purpose. Baptists continually wrestle with the challenge to develop a polity devoted to congregational freedom that will have sufficient unity and order to carry out an effective Christian witness today.

THE BAPTIST MOVEMENT

Baptists in America trace their spiritual roots back through the colonies to Britain. Those roots extend back through the early Baptists to the Separatists whose roots are anchored in the early Celtic Christians who, separated from the continent, developed many of the characteristics of the free church.

A movement toward conformity arose within the Roman Catholic church. As its influence spread, religious liberty was restricted. The freer practices of the Celtic Christians went underground. Eventually there were those in Britain who sought freedom to separate from the control of first the Roman Catholic church and then the Church of England.

British Baptists created a movement that has spread throughout the world. Baptists in America gathered churches in Rhode Island, then in Pennsylvania, New Jersey, and Virginia. Baptist churches in America trace their roots back through these churches to Britain. The profiles in this book illustrate the role British Baptists had in establishing a Baptist movement in America. What has happened since then?

BAPTISTS IN THE UNITED KINGDOM [1]

Organized Baptist life in England had two distinct beginnings, the General and the Particular Baptists. In 1611 Thomas Helwys returned from Amsterdam with a small group who, a few years earlier, had sought religious freedom in Holland where they had formed a Separatist church under the leadership of John Smyth. The successors of Helwys and his friends became known as General Baptists. Their church order, previously independent, was modified by the appointment of inter-congregational officials known as "Messengers."

In 1633 a group connected with a Separatist church in London with Calvinist leanings broke away over the issue of the baptism of believers to form the Particular Baptists. They remained Calvinistic in theology but more independent in their church order. The first Baptist church in Wales was founded in 1649 at Ilston, near Swansea by John Myles. Baptists were in Ireland by the mid-seventeenth century and in Scotland by the mid-eighteenth century. A "New Connexion" of the more evangelical General Baptists was formed in 1770 under the influence of the Methodist revival. The majority of the remaining General Baptist churches became Unitarian.

During the late eighteenth century under the influence of Andrew Fuller and others, there was a resurgence of evangelistic zeal amongst the Particular Baptists. The formation of the Baptist Missionary Society in 1792, whose first missionary, William Carey, went to India in 1793, came from this movement. These Baptist churches rallied around the mission movement and formed in 1812-13 the first Baptist Union. The Union had an uncertain early history, but after its re-formation in 1831-32, Baptists began to draw together. In 1891 the General Baptists of the New Connexion, under the leadership of John Clifford, merged with the Baptist Union. In 1993 the majority of churches in the Old Baptist Union joined the Baptist Union of Great Britain.

The Baptist movement has, over the years, spread to many lands and is today one of the largest Protestant communions in the world. In 1905 Baptist churches came together to form the Baptist World Alliance.

BAPTISTS IN THE UNITED STATES [2]

Baptist Churches in the United States grew out of those first struggling churches in Rhode Island. Religious liberty was the key and the baptism of believers by immersion was the visible sign of the gathered congregation. Calvinism was a strong influence until the late eighteenth century when enthusiasm developed for evangelism and overseas missionary work. Baptists today often stress soul freedom, evangelism and discipleship.

Separation of church and state, adopted by Rhode Island in their charter, was slow to be accepted by the other colonies. It took Massachusetts 150 years.

In 1707 the Philadelphia Baptist Association formed, comprised of five congregations in New Jersey and Pennsylvania. It was agreed the association would honor the autonomy of member churches, while serving as advisors in ordination and conflict.

In the late 18th century Isaac Backus, of Middleborough, Massachusetts, challenged the notion that Baptists (and other Christian groups) still had to pay taxes to support the state church (Congregational).

Other Baptists confronted the issue in the South, where Anglican influences were prominent. In most cases progress was slow. John Leland, a pastor from Virginia, actively supported Thomas Jefferson's religious freedom bill passed in Virginia in 1786. Working with James Madison, Leland was influential in creating the First Amendment to the Constitution: "Congress shall make no law respecting an establishment of religion, or prohibiting the free exercise thereof...."

Baptists have had a passion for mission. The roots of our mission organizations may be traced to the British Missionary Society which was created to give active support to its first missionary, William Carey, in India. In 1812 Adoniram and Ann Judson set sail for India as Congregationalists and arrived as Baptists. In 1814 Luther Rice and others joined to form the General Missionary Convention of the Baptist Denomination in the United States for Foreign Missions (Triennial Convention) to support this new mission.

In 1845 with the slavery issue at a peak Baptists split North and South. The Southern Baptist Convention was formed in the South while the Baptists in the North remained organized as a group of societies, eventually forming the Northern Baptist Convention in 1907.

In 1824 the Baptist General Tract Society was founded. Judson Press has its roots in that society. In 1832 John Mason Peck and Isaac McCoy helped form the Home Mission Society to provide a ministry with Native Americans and the founding of educational institutions. I served a church in Alton, Illinois that was organized by John Mason Peck. The Ministers and Missionaries Benefit Board, founded in 1913, was started in order to meet medical, insurance and pension needs of ordained and lay church workers. It now serves a variety of Baptist organizations.

AMERICAN BAPTIST CHURCHES, USA

You may recall in the prologue that I mentioned I began this as a rather personal journal that would trace not only Baptist beginnings in general, but also my own personal faith roots. Here is where my particular branch of Baptists begins to take shape.

In 1907 the Northern Baptist Convention was formed to coordinate of the work of the foreign, national, and educational societies. The Northern Baptist Convention was renamed in 1950 The American Baptist Convention and then in

1972 it became The American Baptist Churches, U.S.A. The first association formed in 1707 has grown to 35 regions each with its own associations. The national center for the denomination has been located in Valley Forge, Pennsylvania since 1962.

American Baptists always have been actively engaged in ecumenical ministry, both locally and in such bodies as the National Council of Churches of Christ, World Council of Churches and Baptist World Alliance.

BAPTISTS TODAY

Baptists have been called to be "a Christ-centered people" and to return to their roots (the Latin *radix* means roots) by becoming radical disciples. Radical discipleship calls us to be a people of prayer, purpose, and passion seeking the renewal of our ministry and mission.

The British Baptists adopted Five Core Values for a Gospel People. They include the call to be a prophetic, inclusive, sacrificial, missionary, and worshiping community. One way to honor our pioneers is to be as faithful and loyal to our vision today as they were to theirs.

REFLECTIONS - Making a Difference - Galatians 5:13-15 [3]

Baptists have made a difference in the lives of people in the past and we still have the potential to do so today. The dream of making a difference has not died. We are called to reaffirm the cause and to renew the dream. The cause is Christ and the dream is of a better world for all God's children. Let us renew our commitment to the cause of Christ and to the dream of making this a better world in which we all may live.

The serious issue before us today is the cause for which Baptists have stood in their finest hours, the cause that keeps our movement young, and makes it, in its third century, one of the longest lasting associations of Christians in our country.

Our cause has been, since the days of Thomas Helwys, the cause of freedom. Our commitment has been, since the days of Andrew Fuller and William Carey, to share the Good News freely with all who have never known the love of God in their lives. On this foundation we have defined our values, refined our policies, and refreshed our faith. Let us together reaffirm that cause and renew that commitment today.

It is the glory and the greatness of our tradition to speak for those who have no voice, to remember those who are forgotten, to respond to the frustrations and fulfill the dreams of all who seek a better life under the guidance of God. We dare not forsake that tradition. We cannot let the great purposes of Baptists become just a part of history. We must not permit these dreams to die.

We recognize that each generation has a rendezvous with a different reality. The answers of one generation become the questions of the next. But Christ is our guiding star; and again and again, Baptists have followed that star and they have given new meaning to the old values of faith, hope, and love, of freedom and justice for all. Baptists in the past have made a difference; may our dream be that we may be also.

Warren Mild wrote, "Baptists learned that liberty is more important than doctrinal conformity. Hardly realizing what they had been blundering into, they themselves, who in the past as a people had endured so much for religious liberty, had come very close to restricting liberty by insisting upon unanimity of belief among their own members." [4]

May we move ahead with prayer, purpose, and passion and not fight among ourselves, remembering Paul's warning, "My friends, you were chosen to be free. So don't use your freedom as an excuse to do anything you want. Use it as an opportunity to serve each other with love. All that the Law says can be summed up in the command to love others as much as you love yourself. But if you keep attacking each other, you had better watch out or you will destroy yourselves" (Gal. 5:13-15).

Together we can make a difference! Let us move forward in the knowledge that God will be with us on the journey. There will be setbacks and sacrifices, but I am convinced that we are ready to give something back to God in return for all God has given us. We come, as he came, that all might have life, life in all its fullness, abundant life (John 10:10). My dream is, as perhaps it is yours, that in some small way we may make a difference in the lives we touch.

CLOSING

In the Rutgers University chapel one evening years ago as a student I heard Robert Frost, that old New England poet, read in a gravely voice his poem about stopping in the woods for awhile but moving on because he had promises to keep, and miles to go before he would sleep. We have miles to before we sleep - for the work goes on, the cause endures, the hope still lives, and **the dream shall never die.**

Endnotes

Introduction

1. Bruce Reed Pullen, *Discovering Celtic Christianity* (Mystic, CT: Twenty-Third Publications, 1999), p. 111.
2. Alice Blackwell Lewis, *Hopewell Valley Heritage* (Hopewell, New Jersey: Hopewell Museum, 1973), p. 8.
3. David Gates, "Founding Fathers: John Adams Is in the House," *Newsweek*, May 21, 2001, p. 58.

Part One: Prologue

1. Bruce L. Shelley, *Church History in Plain Language* (Waco, Texas: Word, 1982), p. 11

Chapter One

1. Catherine Johns, *Christianity in Roman Britain*, British Museum Magazine, # 36 (2000), p. 18.

Chapter Two

1. Shelley, p.256.
2. Shelley, p. 272.
3. J. Brent Walker, *Report from the Capital*, Vol. 55, No. 8.
4. Richard of Chichester, "Day by Day" in *Famous Prayers*, ed. Veronica Zundel (Grand Rapids, Michigan: Eerdmans Publishing Company, 1984), p.31.

Part Two: Profiles

1. Maxie Dunnam, *The Communicator's Commentary: Galatians, Ephesians, Philippians, Colossians, Philemon.* (Waco, Texas: Word, 1982), p.376

Chapter Three

1. Thomas Helwys, *A Declaration of Faith* (Amsterdam, 1611) quoted by B.R.White, *The English Baptists of the 17th Century* (Didcot, England: Baptist Historical Society, 1996), p. 213.

2. Thomas Helwys, *A Short Declaration of the Mystery of Iniquity* (London, 1612) quoted in *Baptist Roots* (Valley Forge: Judson Press, 1999), p. 86.

3. Thomas Helwys, (original copy as found in the Duke Humfrey's Library at Oxford), p.6.

Chapter Four

1. Muriel James, *Religious Liberty on Trial. Hanserd Knollys - Early Baptist Hero.* (Franklin, Tennessee: Providence House Publishers, 1997), p. 68.

2. James, p. 131

3. James, p. 185.

Chapter Five

1. H. Leon McBeth, *The Baptist Heritage* (Nashville: Broadman Press, 1987), p. 131.

2. *An Historical Note*, Pembroke College, Cambridge, October 1984.

3. James Ernst, *Roger Williams - New England Firebrand* (New York: Macmillan, 1932), p. 443.

Chapter Six

1. Bill Leonard, *Baptist Ways: A History* (Valley Forge: Judson Press, 2003)p. 77.

2. Wilbur Nelson, *The Life of Dr. John Clarke* (Newport: First Baptist John Clarke Memorial Church, 1924. Fifth printing, 1983), p.15.

3. Louis Asher, *John Clarke (1609-1676).* (Pittsburgh: Dorrance Publishing, 1997), p.101-102.

Chapter Seven

1. Samuel Eliot Morison, *Three Centuries of Harvard* (Cambridge: Harvard University Press, 1936), p. 11.

2. Samuel Eliot Morison, *Harvard in the Seventeenth Century* (Cambridge: Harvard University, 1936), p. 319.

3. Jeremiah Chaplin, *Life of Henry Dunster - First President of Harvard College* (Boston: James Osgood, 1872), pp. 99-100.

4. Chaplin, p. 65.

Chapter Eight

1, Covenant used at Calvary Baptist Church, Hopewell, NJ, 1971.

Chapter Nine

1. John Bunyan, *The Pilgrim's Progress - Part Two*, 1684.

2. Anne Arnott, *Valiant for Truth - The Story of John Bunyan* (Grand Rapids, Michigan: Eerdmans Publishing Company, 1986), p. 155.

3. John Bunyan, *The Pilgrim's Progress* (London: Nathaniel Ponder, 1678). Heritage Press edition, 1942, pp. 48-9.

Chapter Ten

1. Timothy George and David S. Dockery, editors. *Baptist Theologians* (Nashville: Broadman, 1990), p.68.

Chapter Eleven

1. Stephen Bernard Nutter, *The Story of the Cambridge Baptists and the Struggle for Religious Liberty* (Cambridge: Heffer & Sons, 1912), p. 160.

2. David Bebbington, *Evangelicalism in Modern Britain* (Grand Rapids: Baker Book House, 1992), p. 63.

3. Bebbington, p. 65

4. Andrew Fuller, *Works* (London, 1837) as found in Roger Hayden, "The Life and Influence of Andrew Fuller" in *The Kettering Connection - Northamptonshire Baptists and Overseas Missions*, edited by R. L. Greenall (Leicester: Department of Adult Education, University of Leicester, 1993), p. 8.

5. Fuller, *Works* IV, 20. From Hayden, p. 7.

Chapter Twelve

1. Nutter, p. 165.

2. Nutter, p. 165

3. Mike Nicholls, *C.H. Spurgeon - The Pastor Evangelist* (Didcot, England: Baptist Historical Soc., 1992), p. 37.

4. Geoff Thomas, "The Preacher's Progress," in *Marvelous Ministry*, edited by Timothy George (Ligonier, PA: Soli Deo Gloria Publications, 1993), p. 48

5. Thomas, p. 51.

6. Louis Drummond, "Introduction" to Charles Haddon Spurgeon, *The Quotable Spurgeon* (Wheaton, Illinois: Harold Shaw Publishers, 1990). Excerpts from Feathers for Arrows by C.H. Spurgeon (Clapham, 1870), p. vii

7. James T. Allen, Life Story of C. H. Spurgeon (Albany, OR: Sage Digital Library, 1996), p, 42.

Part Three: Epilogue (Chapter 13)

1. *Baptists in the United Kingdom,* from an annual report of the Baptist Union, p. 39. (revised by the author)

2. *American Baptists - A Brief History,* from the American Baptist Churches - USA website. (edited by the author)

3. Bruce Pullen, sermon preached to the General Board, November 1984. (excerpts taken from it)

4. Warren Mild. *The Story of the American Baptists - The Role of a Remnant* (Valley Forge: Board of Educational Ministries, 1976), p. 62.

Early Christian sign
British Museum
Alpha-Omega
Chi Rho

Guidebooks for the Journey

A Selected Bibliography

1. Celtic Roots

Christianity in Roman Britain. London: British Museum Magazine. Number 36. Spring 2000.

Edwards, Brian and Clive Anderson. *Through the British Museum - with the Bible*. Leominster, England: Day One Publications, 2004.

Hunter, George. *The Celtic Way of Evangelism – How Christianity can reach the West...Again.* Nashville: Abingdon Press, 2000.

Pullen, Bruce. *Discovering Celtic Christianity*. Mystic, Connecticut: Twenty-Third Publications, 1999.

2. The Cross and the Crown

Marshall, David. *Pilgrim Ways*. Grantham, England: Autumn House, 1993.

Wright, John Christopher. *A Guide to the Pilgrims' Way and North Downs Way*. London: Constable & Company, 1971. 4th edition, 1993. (Both specific to the Pilgrims' Way)

3. Thomas Helwys

Petroski, Henry. *The Book on the Book Shelf.* New York: Alfred Knopf, 1999. (Specific reference to the Bodleian - Duke Humphrey's Library)

4. Hanserd Knollys

Haykin, Michael. *Rediscovering our English Baptist Heritage-Kiffin, Knollys and Keach*. Leeds, England: Reformation Today Trust, 1996

James, Muriel. *Religious Liberty on Trial. Hanserd Knolly -Early Baptist Hero.* Franklin, Tennessee: Providence House Publishers, 1997.

5. Roger Williams

Ernst, James. *Roger Williams.* New York: The Macmillan Company, 1932.

Gaustad, Edwin S. *Liberty of Conscience - Roger Williams in America.* Valley Forge: Judson Press, 1999.

Lemons, J. Stanley. *The First Baptist Church in America.* Providence, Rhode Island: Charitable Baptist Society, 1988.

6. John Clarke

Asher, Louis Franklin. *John Clarke (1609-1676).* Pittsburgh: Dorrance Publishing Co.,Inc. 1997

Nelson, Wilbur. *The Hero of Aquidneck - A Life of Dr. John Clarke.* New York: Fleming Revell, 1938. Third Printing, December 1998 by the John Clarke Trust.

7. Henry Dunster

Chaplin, Jeremiah. *Life of Henry Dunster - First President of Harvard College.* Boston: James R. Osgood and Co., 1872.

Morison, Samuel Eliot. *Harvard in the Seventeenth Century.* Cambridge: Harvard University Press, 1936.

8. John Myles

Brush, John Woolman. *Baptists in Massachusetts.* Valley Forge: Judson Press, 1970.

Gregor, Gary, *John Miles: Gower's "Pilgrim Father"* found in Gower, Volume XLVI. Swansea, Wales: The Journal of the Gower Society, 1995.

9. John Bunyan

Arnott, Anne. *Valiant for Truth - The Story of John Bunyan.* Grand Rapids, Michigan: Wm. B. Eerdmans Publishing Co., 1985. In England as *He Shall with Giants Fight.*

10. Benjamin Keach

George, Timothy and David S. Dockery, editors. *Baptist Theologians*. Benjamin Keach by J. Barry Vaughn. (p. 49-76). Nashville: Broadman Press, 1990.

Martin, Hugh, *Benjamin Keach - Pioneer of Congregational Hymn Singing*. London: Independent Press, 1961.

11. Andrew Fuller

Butlin, Ashley and Jenny. *Fuller Baptist Church - An Outline History 1696-1991*. Norwich: Coorlea Publishing.

Greenall, R. L., editor. *The Kettering Connection - Northamptonshire Baptists and Overseas Missions*. Leicester, England: University of Leicester, 1993.

12. Charles Haddon Spurgeon

Day, Richard Ellsworth. *The Shadow of the Broad Brim – The Life-Story of Charles Haddon Spurgeon: Heir of the Puritans*. Philadelphia: The Judson Press, 1934.

Curnow, Tim; Errol Hulse, David Kingdom, and Geoff Thomas. *A Marvelous Ministry - How the All-round Ministry of C H Spurgeon Speaks to Us Today*. Ligonier, PA: Soli Deo Gloria Publications, 1993.

Drummond, Lewis. *Spurgeon - Prince of Preachers*. Grand Rapids: Kregel Publications, 1992.

Nicholls, Mike. *C. H. Spurgeon - The Pastor Evangelist*. Didcot, Oxford: Baptist Historical Soceity, 1992.

13. May the Dream Never Die

Five Core Values. The Baptist Union of Great Britain, Baptist House, P. O. Box 44, 129 Broadway, Didcot, Oxfordshire, OX11 8RT, England (web: www.baptist.org.uk).

American Baptist Churches USA. (www.abc-usa.org)

Cooperative Baptist Fellowship. (www.thefellowship.info)

BOOKS ON BAPTISTS IN GENERAL

American Baptist Quarterly, The American Baptist Historical
Society, Valley Forge, PA.

> 1. *Baptist Issues During the Colonial Era.* Volume XXII.
> Number 4. December, 2003.

> 2. *John Bunyan: A Tercentenary.* Volume VII. Number 4.
> December, 1988.

Brackney, William. *Baptist Life and Thought: 1600-1980 – A
Source Book.* Valley Forge: Judson Press, 1983.

Brackney, William. Special issue editor. *The Baptists – A People
who gathered "to walk in all His ways."* Worcester, PA,
Christian History Magazine, 1985. Volume 4, Number 2.

Freeman, Curtis; James Wm. McClendon, Jr., and C. Rosalee
Velloso da Silva. *Baptist Roots - A Reader in the Theology of a
Christian People.* Valley Forge: Judson Press, 1999. (Thomas
Helwys, John Bunyan, Roger Williams, Andrew Fuller,
Charles H. Spurgeon).

George, Timothy and David S. Dockery. *Baptist Theologians.*
Nashville: Broadman Press, 1990. (John Bunyan, Benjamin
Keach, Andrew Fuller, Charles Spurgeon)

HISTORIES

Brown, Raymond. *The English Baptists of the Eighteenth Century.*
London: The Baptist Historical Society, 1986.

Evans, B. *Early English Baptists.* London: J. Heaton & Sons, 1862.
Reprinted 1977 by Attic Press, Inc. Greenwood, S.C.

McBeth, H. Leon. *The Baptist Heritage - Four Centuries of Baptist
Witness.* Nashville: Broadman Press, 1987.

Robinson, H. Wheeler. *The Life and Faith of the Baptists.* London,
1946; and Payne, Ernest.

*The Fellowship of Believers - Baptist Thought and Practice
Yesterday and Today.* London, 1952. Reprinted in New York
under the title *British Baptists* by Arno Press, 1980.

Shelley, Bruce. *Church History in Plain Language.* Waco, Texas:
Word Books, 1982.

Torbet, Robert. *A History of the Baptists*. Valley Forge: Judson, 1963.

White, B. R. *The English Baptists of the Seventeenth Century*. Didcot, England: The Baptist Historical Society, 1996.

TALES WE TELL ALONG THE WAY

For Reflection and Small Group Discussion

Pilgrimages are often best taken with friends, so invite your friends to read this book and discuss it with you around the kitchen table; or organize a study group in your home, church, school, or place of work and share your stories. Take a pilgrimage together as you discover your Baptist roots. The publisher, InfinityPublishing.com, offers significant discounts for groups that wish to purchase for resale. Shipping on 20 copies is free.

My experience has been that if you have a morning group it is best to start with something to drink, often coffee, or juice, and something light to eat, such as cookies. Evening groups often work best when refreshments are served afterwards. Whatever time of day or schedule you choose, make this a fun and welcoming time.

Help for studying the Scripture text in each chapter can be found in the Serendipity Bible or in LESSON maker 4 for Windows, a computer program developed by NavPress Software (1934 Rutland Drive, Suite 500, Austin Texas 78758) to create outlines for small group sessions.

Below are some questions to prime personal reflection or group discussion. The first question is a discussion starter, the second deals with the scripture, the third with how we might respond. For group discussions you may wish to combine chapters 1-2, 3-5, 6-7, 8-9, 10-11, and 12-13 to make six sessions.

QUESTIONS FOR CHAPTER 1. Luke 10:1-8

1. What difficult task have you done recently? How did you feel when you completed it?
2. Why does Jesus ask us to pray for more workers? What instructions did he give his followers? When they returned, what did they report happened? What should give them joy?
3. What does this story encourage us to do? Have you ever tried to tell someone about Jesus? What happened?

QUESTIONS FOR CHAPTER 2. Leviticus 25:8-17

1. What is the most meaningful celebration you participate in each year?
2. What was supposed to be the significance of celebrating the Year of Jubilee? (25:8-17)
3. How do we celebrate our religious freedom? (Day/ activity?)

QUESTIONS FOR CHAPTER 3. Acts 8: 26-40.

1. Who was one of your best teachers? Tell us about her or him?
2. Why had the official gone to Jerusalem? What was his problem? How did Philip help? How did he respond to what Philip said?
3. In what ways can your church reach out to the people in your community? Why are some parts of the Bible difficult to understand? Where can we get help understanding the Bible better? What fears prevent us from telling others about Jesus? What is one thing you can do to overcome your fears in sharing your faith?

Try writing out what you would say to someone (like the official) who asks you to tell him about what Jesus means to you so that you will be prepared when the Spirit leads you to invite someone to follow Jesus.

QUESTIONS FOR 4. Acts 26:12-16;

1. What is one story from your past that you enjoy telling?
2. How did Paul describe his conversion and new life? (26:12-18). What was Paul's primary goal in his speech? How did Paul tailor his message to the audience he faced?
3. How can we use stories of our own experience to share the message of Christ? Why is it important to pray for your political leaders? Give some examples of toleration and intoleration in our society. (Perhaps you could find an article that would illustrate the example in a newspaper or news magazine).

QUESTIONS FOR 5. Amos 5:18-24.

1. If suddenly you inherited a lot of money, what would you do?
2. What did Amos tell them God did not like? What did he tell the people to do?

3. If your behavior was troubling to others, which family member would do the best job of advising you? If Amos visited your congregation, what examples of religious hypocrisy might he point out? How can you share some of your resources with those who are needy or oppressed?

QUESTIONS FOR 6. Mark 1:5-11.

1. How do you show approval of others? When were you affirmed by someone?

2. What mental image comes to mind when you hear the word "baptism"? Why was this event significant? (1:9). What happened after Jesus was baptized? (1:10) What did the voice from heaven say about Jesus? (1:11)

3. How should we respond to Jesus' example of baptism? What does it mean for someone to call his or her way of life a ministry? Do we assume a new way of life after we are baptized? How are repentance, baptism, forgiveness, prayer, the Holy Spirit's presence, and God's blessing all important in your life as a Christian?

QUESTIONS FOR CHAPTER 7. Psalm 1

1. When has peer pressure influenced your attitudes or actions? What's most important to you about your friendships with Christians?

2. What are the main points the psalm writer makes in this poem? (1:1-6) What does the image of the tree tell us about the righteous person? (1:3) What does this psalm teach us about spiritual discipline? What kind of "fruit" should we yield?

3. How do you practice meditating on the Bible? What attitude or action would you like to cultivate (work on) in your life this month? What Christian book have you read recently?

QUESTIONS FOR CHAPTER 8. Hebrews 10:16-25

1. Recall a time in your life when in the face of an extremely difficult situation, you hung in there.

2. What did Jesus dying accomplish for those who would trust in Him? (10:14) Why did the author say that those under the new covenant could draw near to God? (10:19-22) Why are Christians able to hold on in following Jesus? (10:23) What kind of behavior

should believers demonstrate toward one another? (10:24-25). What influences the ups and downs in your spiritual journey?

3. What encourages you to love and do good? Is yours a covenant driven church? Does your church have a covenant? Do you understand it? Is it a generic covenant? Does your church's covenant need to be revised and rewritten based on your particular congregation's understanding of its ministry and mission?

QUESTIONS FOR CHAPTER 9. Luke 1:1-4

1. What period in history do you wish you could visit? Why?

2. How had Luke received his evidence? On whom did Luke rely for his information? (Luke 1:2). How did Luke describe his approach to historical research? What reasons did Luke give for deciding to write his Gospel? (1:3-4). What did he hope would be the result of this Gospel (1:4)

3. Were people of Luke's day better observers, listeners, and witnesses than people today?

4. What makes you certain of the things you were taught? Why is *Pilgrim's Progress*, which describes a way to God, such a powerful evangelical witness? Try writing about a faith experience of yours and then sharing it with a friend.

QUESTIONS FOR CHAPTER 10. Psalm 98:4-6

1. How do you celebrate special days or events in your family? In what ways does sharing a meal bind people together?

2. Matthew 26:26-30. What did Jesus say about the bread on the table? What remarks did Jesus make about the wine they were drinking? When did Jesus say He would eat with His disciples again? What did the group do after they finished eating?

3. Psalm 98:4-6. What specific instructions does this psalm offer about how to worship God? What imagery is used to described the whole world's praise to God?

4. What has this psalm taught you about joy? How can we keep our spiritual lives fresh and exciting? What is one step you could take to add new meaning to your worship of God? How can we guard against getting into a rut in our spiritual journeys?

QUESTIONS FOR CHAPTER 11. Isaiah 2:1-4 and 54:2-3

1. What comes to your mind when you think of a perfect world?
2. In Isaiah's vision, who will look up to the Lord in the last days? (2:1-3). What will be the status of international relations then? (2:4). What did Isaiah predict for God's kingdom in terms of numbers and prosperity? (54:2-3).
3. What would have to change in order for people to feel that they no longer needed weapons? Why do we tend to put our trust in people rather than in God? How can we best advocate and support mission in the new millennium?

QUESTIONS FOR CHAPTER 12. Acts 16:25-34

1. Has anyone ever asked you, "How may I be saved?" If so, what did you tell them?
2. What happened while Paul and Silas were praying and singing hymns? (16:25-26) What were the results of the talk Paul and Silas had with the jailer? (16:31-34)
3. What can a Christian do to be prepared for persecution? When in your experience has the Lord provided a happy ending to a bad turn of events? What can we learn from Paul and Silas to help us cope with difficult times ahead? How can you encourage someone else in his or her Christian walk this week?
4. Not everyone can be a greater preacher, but great listeners help create good preachers. Try taking notes of a sermon so that you might recall and meditate on its message during the week.

QUESTIONS FOR CHAPTER 13. Gal. 5:13-15, John 10:1-10.

1. What kind of games do you play? Do they have many or few rules? Do you create new rules of play?
2. How did Paul ask the Galatians to use their freedom? What was his warning? Jesus warned his followers that there would be those who would come and lead them astray? Can you cite some examples? How has Jesus made your life richer?
3. What are some of your dreams for a better life? For yourself? For your family? For your church? For your community? What are your core values? What are the ministries to which people are called in your congregation?

PLACES ALONG THE WAY

Travel Notes

Most of the places mentioned in our travels are easily found on their website. Traveling in Britain (for those from the states) and in the United States (for those in Britain) is very similar. Just stay out of the big cities and their traffic until you become familiar with driving on the other side of the road. If you are traveling to Britain and plan to drive, spring is a good time of year to go. Hotel, air and car packages are more reasonable then. Check American or British Airlines packages.

The British Museum, London. We stayed at the Bonnington Hotel in Bloomsbury, 92 Southampton Row, Holborn, within walking distance of the museum. Parking is a problem in London so do not drive in the city. If renting a car to visit other sites in Britain, Wales or Scotland, pick the car up after visiting the city sites or drop it off after visiting other parts of Britain and before touring the city.

The Metropolitan Tabernacle, Southwark (London). You may wish to visit the church made famous by Charles Spurgeon. Services are at 11 on Sundays. After stopping there, you might visit the Southwark Cathedral where John Harvard was baptized and the famous London Eye Ferris wheel.

Spurgeon's College, 189 S. Norwood Hill, London SE25 6DJ. Visit the Heritage Room above the chapel. Contact Judy Powles, the librarian ahead of time.

Iona, Scotland. We stayed with Jennie McCellan at *Dun Craig.* Isle of Iona, Argyll PA76 6SP, Scotland. This is a small Christian retreat house, reasonably priced. You are not allowed to bring cars on the island unless you are handicapped. Even then you must have special permission obtained ahead of time.

It is worth staying over night during the summer for a couple of days in order to participate in the worship services and activities of this small isolated island that is so filled with tradition.

Swansea, Wales. We stayed at the Nicholaston House outside of Swansea overlooking the Three Cliffs area, one of the five finest scenic places in Britain. It is a Christian counseling center. The facilities are excellent. The center has programs on weekends but often has rooms available during the week. The Ilston memorial to the first Baptist church in Wales, founded by John Myles, is nearby. Contact Derek and Anne Styants, Penmaen, Goer, Swansea SA3 2HL (01792 371317).

Visit the Pen Gwydr Baptist Church in Swansea on Sunday. The Dylan Thomas center is also here in Swansea.

South Wales Baptist College, 54-58 Richmond Road, Cardiff, Wales CF2 3UR. One of several colleges preparing Baptist pastors. Check out Cardiff Castle and the Museum of Welsh Life while there. **Cambrensis**, a Christian chorus, has their annual concert in Cardiff in May. Check out their web-site. We have been twice. Thrilling music provided by a core choir of fifty and supplemented by church choristers and an orchestra.

St. Davids, Wales. If you are vacationing in Wales the last week in May, St. Davids cathedral offers a menu of classical concerts.

Winchester Cathedral, Winchester. We stayed at the Royal Hotel, St. Peter Street. Originally built as a private house, it was used from 1794 by a group of nuns who had fled Brussels. In 1857 it became a hotel. There is a lovely garden, a small restaurant, and excellent service.

Canterbury Cathedral and St. Augustine's Abbey, Canterbury. We stayed with John and Anne Davies in their B&B, Magnolia House, 36 Dunston's Terrace in Canterbury, Kent CT2 8AX. It is within walking distance of the cathedral. The English Tourism Council Gold Award winner, it "has all the comfort and warm welcome pilgrims dream of."

Cambridge: Pembroke, St. Catharine's, and Magdalen Colleges. All have web-sites. If you want a tour guide, arrange it ahead of time. Exams in the spring often mean visitors are not allowed on the grounds. Little Gidding (made famous by T.S. Eliot) and its old chapel are nearby. It is an adventure finding it.

Fuller Baptist Church in Kettering (Andrew Fuller). We contacted archivist, John Premble. 70 St. Mary's Road, Kettering NN15 7BW who showed us the site where the British Missionary Society was formed and the heritage room at the church.

Baptist Churches in the United States.

Hopewell, New Jersey - church is closed. John Hart, signer of the Declaration of Independence is buried here.

First Baptist Church, Providence, Rhode Island. The secretary will provide a self-guided tour of the building. If you arrive during the week, ask her about parking out back.

United Baptist Church in Newport, Rhode Island. Contact the pastor ahead of time to visit the heritage room. While in Newport visit the grand summer homes and the waterfront.

Baptist Polity and Identity

The author wrote *Profiles in Faith - Discovering Baptist Beginnings* out of the concern that we not forget the heroes of our faith who helped shaped who we are today as Baptists. He was a member of the team that drafted, out of a concern for our Baptist polity (the process of how we govern ourselves) and Baptist identity (the characteristics that shape our identity), a statement to be submitted to the 2007 Biennial in Washington, D.C. **This is an excerpt from that document.**

American Baptist Churches - Our Polity and Identity

American Baptist Churches are unique. Though congregations are different there are many similarities. Our roots reach back through the colonies to Britain and beyond where the first Christians began developing the convictions that have led to our being called Baptists. Our distinctive Baptist identification lies in our polity which is based upon our theology and faith beliefs.

Polity includes the process by which we embrace congregational representation that allows us to organize ourselves and function together in association within the American Baptist Churches USA. We take seriously our polity, though challenged by congregational autonomy, which allows us to have sufficient unity and order to carry out an effective Christian witness as American Baptists.

OUR CONVICTIONS

Based upon the Word of God and guided in scriptural understanding by the Holy Spirit, American Baptists have gathered to worship, seek God's will for their lives and actively live out their faith in the world. American Baptists are a people who do not require conformity to a particular creedal position or statement of faith. We do, however, acknowledge some common convictions that characterize what we believe. Some convictions are held in common with other Christians and some uniquely characterize Baptists.

Many American Baptists hold these convictions in common with other Christians:

The Trinity, believing in God as Creator, Jesus as Lord and Savior, and the Holy Spirit as God's presence in and among us.

The Bible is the divinely inspired Word of God in its original manuscripts. It serves as the final written authority for living out the Christian faith through the guidance of the Holy Spirit as interpreted within the community of believers.

Salvation is through faith alone in Jesus Christ. Good works are an outward manifestation of a changed life in Jesus.

The Great Commandment and Commission, believing we are called to love God and love people, and to enable people to become disciples, part of the church through baptism, and to witness to what we believe to the ends of the earth.

These convictions characterize American Baptists:

Believer's baptism by immersion rather than infant baptism.

Believers should be mature enough to make a valid profession of faith.

The gathered church rather than a parish church.

The separation of church and state. We support religious freedom and respect the expressions of faith of others.

The Priesthood of Believers, believing all persons are equal before God.

Soul Freedom, believing each person is responsible for the condition of his or her own soul before God.

The ordinances of Baptism and the Lord's Supper as commanded by Jesus Christ for implementation within the church body.

Autonomy of the local church.

The local church as the fundamental unit of mission in denominational life.

-Finis-